Developing Physical Heal
Well-being through Gymnas
(5–7)

How can you make gymnastics activity fun, lively and inclusive?

How can you improve the health and well-being of all your children?

How can you ensure progression over time?

This practical and easy-to-use teacher's guide is the brand new edition of the popular workbook *Movement Education Leading to Gymnastics 4–7*. It takes a session-by-session approach to teaching physical development and well-being through gymnastics for the 5–7 age range.

Fully updated with the most current schemes of work to use at Key Stage 1, it sets out a series of 40 sessions over the two year span, to give you planned and logical progression of both content and advice.

This one-stop resource includes 20 session plans per year group, which you can follow as a complete course or dip into for ideas and inspiration. It also includes a Specific Skills Guide to help you support children in developing the correct techniques.

Each session plan includes:

- Learning objectives
- Apparatus needed
- Warm-up and cool-down activities
- Step-by-step session content
- Teaching approaches
- Assessment criteria
- Health and Safety considerations.

The companion volume, *Developing Physical Health, Fitness and Well-being through Gymnastics 7–11*, follows the same format and together these user-friendly books provide a progressive programme of work from Years 1–6. If you are a practising or student teacher, this guide will give you all the confidence you need to teach gymnastics in your school!

Maggie Carroll retired from her post as Head of the School of Education at the University of Brighton, UK in 2004. Since this time she has worked in a freelance consultative capacity, in addition to her role as Associate Lecturer in Education Studies at Brighton.

Jackie Hannay is currently the Course Leader of BA (Hons) Education Key Stage 2/3 course with QTS and Principal Lecturer in the School of Education at the University of Brighton, UK.

Developing Physical Health and Well-being through Gymnastic Activity (5–7)

A session-by-session approach

Second edition

Maggie Carroll
and Jackie Hannay

LONDON AND NEW YORK

First edition published 1991
by RoutledgeFalmer

This second edition published 2011
by Routledge
2 Park Square, Milton Park, Abingdon, Oxon OX14 4RN

Simultaneously published in the USA and Canada
by Routledge
270 Madison Avenue, New York, NY 10016

Routledge is an imprint of the Taylor & Francis Group, an informa business

Typeset in Bembo, Frutiger and Futura by
Florence Production Ltd, Stoodleigh, Devon
Printed and bound in Spain by
Grafos, Barcelona

British Library Cataloguing in Publication Data
A catalogue record for this book is available from the British Library

Library of Congress Cataloging-in-Publication Data
Carroll, M. E.
    Developing physical health and well-being through gymnastic
    activity (5–7): a session-by-session approach/Maggie Carroll and
    Jackie Hannay.—2nd ed.
        p. cm.
    1. Gymnastics for children.   2. Movement education.
    I. Hannay, Jackie.   II. Title.
    GV464.5.C342011
    796.44083–dc22   2010022546

ISBN13: 978–0–415–59107–2 (hbk)
ISBN13: 978–0–415–59106–5 (pbk)
ISBN13: 978–0–203–83663–7 (ebk)

Contents

Acknowledgements

Photographs: Les Cross, Principal Technician, University of Brighton

Illustrations: Based on illustrations by Marilyn Amos

Children: Rodmell Church of England Primary School, East Sussex

Preface

Jackie Hannay and I were delighted when asked to write new editions of my original teachers' gymnastics workbooks for primary school teachers and students. (The first series was co-authored by myself and Bob Garner, and the second by myself and Hazel Manners.)

The need for this new edition became self evident for two reasons:

1   The success of the series and its format, as evidenced by ongoing testimonies from teachers and students on its usefulness and clarity.

2   Inevitable changes to the primary curriculum over time have necessitated our re-evaluation of the principles underlying the teaching of gymnastic activity. Many of these still pertain but, additionally, we have focussed more of the work on children's well-being, and on how it also supports access to broad learning across the curriculum.

We have retained a similar format and approach as in the original versions because teachers have told us how this has made their planning and assessment straightforward and manageable.

We welcome this opportunity to share with teachers and students this contribution to a crucial aspect of young children's development.

Maggie Carroll
Jackie Hannay
University of Brighton, September 2010

Foreword

The updating of this book is very welcome. It has always been a most valuable resource for the primary school subject leader, experienced teacher and, especially, the non-specialist. The lesson outlines have a clear structure with a good range of activities that, when sequenced, help learners to develop specific sets of skills and apply them appropriately. The units are well designed with development of core skills, specific techniques and compositional concepts and the ideas central to them. In addition, there is a very clear section in each lesson that helps teachers to know what to look for in terms of specific learning outcomes. The authors also make excellent use of the core tasks developed as part of Curriculum 2000 and, subsequently, the PESSYP strategy.

Carroll and Hannay have skilfully updated the materials in order to reflect both the most recent curriculum developments in physical education and the most up-to-date thinking about teaching and learning. Whatever happens to the National Curriculum, the books will provide a very strong starting point for the development of positive learning experiences in this area of physical education. For subject leaders, they provide an excellent resource to support the development of schemes of work and a 'feel safe', clear set of ideas that can be turned into lesson plans for the non-specialist. For those who use the resource well, it will enable high quality curriculum learning experiences and teaching to be provided for all learners. This will offer the settings in which children, whatever their ability, can develop their:

- physical competency;
- confidence in themselves as physical beings;
- creativity and performance skills; and
- knowledge and understanding of aspects of personal health and well-being, and healthy lifestyles.

Crichton Casbon
Crichton Casbon Consulting Ltd
www.cccreates.co.uk

Introduction

Physical skills develop from the moment children are born. It is during the early years of children's lives (3–7) that physical education (PE) is primarily concerned with physical development. Young children need to be provided with opportunities to explore a range of physical movement and equipment through structured and exploratory play in order to develop and master key motor skills.

Development of these skills will only occur through regular activity during the early, middle and later primary school phases. Whatever form a national curriculum might take for young children, concern for physical development, health and well-being must predominate, and, as such, is vital for children's development as confident individuals. It provides the foundations for long-term well-being and contributes to children's all-round development.

This workbook sets out to ensure that gymnastic activities, as part of a balanced PE programme, offer opportunities for children to acquire aspects of:

- physical skill acquisition and performance that is improved through practice (they will become competent in the control and dexterity of their movements, and will use these abilities creatively and with commitment);

- generic skills so that they can move in controlled ways and in a range of different contexts; and

- broader learning across the curriculum, often related to their personal, emotional and social development.

Therefore, PE in the early years needs to enable children to develop generic skills such as running, throwing, catching, climbing and balancing. From this, they will learn to increase their agility, coordination and strength, and test and challenge themselves, all the time learning what their bodies can do.

They will begin to master natural actions of rolling, climbing, running, jumping and sliding, combined with controlling the weight of the body while moving. These form the basis of a 'gymnastic environment' in which children can progress from moving hesitantly to performing competently with understanding and awareness. They will learn sequences that they are able to replicate and develop towards an optimum performance. They will learn to cooperate and solve problems.

Furthermore, PE sessions focussing on gymnastic activities provide the ideal context for children to develop social skills such as communicating, negotiating, taking the lead and sharing ideas. Also, they will be able to challenge themselves by developing a deepening knowledge of good work. All of this needs to be planned for, and its development supported. For example, to be able to give feedback to another is a sophisticated skill that needs to be nurtured and developed to ensure that it is given in a positive manner, and that it benefits the receiver.

Through the mastery of skills and through achievement, children will be able to develop their sense of worth and well-being. This, combined with the knowledge and understanding of matters such as nutrition, hygiene, sleep and the importance of achieving a balance of these, will allow them to make informed choices and engage in a healthy lifestyle. Children's engagement in gymnastic activities will, in part, provide a framework for them to gain this knowledge and expertise.

Links can be made to other areas of the curriculum in order to enhance children's learning, but these should not be contrived. Indeed, certain areas of PE may lend themselves more appropriately to cross-curricular work, especially in the outside learning environment.

Gymnastic activities develop children's strength, balance, speed, suppleness, stamina and core body skills, as well as posture. These have importance for other areas of the PE programme. For example, to be successful games players, children need to have many of these attributes.

The use of information and computing technology (ICT) has a key part to play in teaching gymnastic activity. In the later section, 'So what about assessment?' (page 6), ICT is considered to be an essential assessment tool that can be used with the children to enable the teacher to capture performances. Together with the teacher, the children will be able to evaluate and celebrate their achievements.

What is involved in gymnastics?

Definitions are often difficult and imprecise. A definition of gymnastics is not necessarily helpful – yet it is necessary to know what characterises the work. It would seem that whatever form gymnastics takes (for example, Olympic, rhythmic, educational, sports, acrobatics, vaulting and agility), certain kinds of attributes give the work its name.

Gymnastics is normally characterised as having components such as:

● physical (strength/flexibility);
● skill (with/without apparatus);
● aesthetic (shape/line/finish);
● creative (choosing/movements);
● cognitive (understanding what the body is doing); and
● psychological (perseverance/courage/determination).

This list, however, need not deter teachers. They do not need to be gymnasts themselves, nor have detailed knowledge of complex gymnastics skills. At Key Stage 1, children should be developing their physical and motor skills through exploring basic movements such as jumping, balancing, travelling, rolling and so on. They should be developing their knowledge of their own physical development, their health and their well-being. In doing so, the characteristic components of gymnastics will gradually emerge as children progress through primary school.

If these characteristics need to be present for the activity to be called 'gymnastics', and if the work is to happen in school, a teaching approach must be adopted throughout that will, on one hand, generate the development of these essential characteristics, and, on the other, will be a relevant educational experience. Children should, therefore, be able to demonstrate bodily skill on the floor, on apparatus, on their own and with a partner, with the ultimate aim of creating a performance.

How do teachers achieve this aim?

It is here that the individual needs of the developing child must be considered. The early phase school child is using 'gymnastic' activities to explore a range of movements – and, in the early stages of development, these are often uncoordinated or uncontrolled, and lacking in dexterity. The role of the teacher, at this stage, is to intervene to make the children *conscious* of what they are doing, so that they are both *moving* and *knowing*. Further to this, the teacher is also developing the children's knowledge of the criteria that they need to consider in order to improve and achieve the desired outcome.

As the children develop through the three phases of development in the primary school years (early, middle and later), the teacher should seek to develop more stylised, skilled bodily actions that have a clearer resemblance to recognised gymnastics forms. By the end of Key Stage 2, children should be capable of demonstrating a range of skilled, controlled and refined body actions combined in a sequence, which they have achieved through selection and a combination of movements (with consideration of levels, speed and direction), assessment and refinement. Through this cycle, children will work towards achieving their ultimate performance.

If gymnastics is about bodily skill (as it undoubtedly is) and we want our children to be proficient in using skilled bodily movement in answer to various kinds of tasks, the style of teaching must operate fully along the methodological continuum of 'open – ended (process) – closed (product)'. It makes sense that some activities require direct teaching, whereas others, particularly in the early years, lend themselves to an experimental approach. Sometimes, the teacher will set tasks that tightly constrain what the children may do (for example, 'run and stop'). At other times, children may need to demonstrate understanding of a movement concept in their performance, and so the task will be of a different order (for example, 'find ways of travelling with your feet together'). There are also many other stages in between that are fairly constraining.

Ultimately, for children to succeed, they need to enjoy gymnastic activities. This can only be achieved by ensuring that every child experiences success, and, therefore, teachers need to cater for individual needs. Children usually respond positively to challenges, and so these need to be built into the sessions to ensure that they are achievable and celebrated. Opportunities to share successes may be extended to outside the class through performing to other classes, in assemblies, to parents and within the community.

Creating a positive ethos in sessions will optimise children's learning. If children feel that their abilities are recognised, that their ideas have been valued and that they are safe, they are more likely to experience a smooth transition to the next Key Stage of their schooling. Gymnastics sessions are well suited to promoting such an ethos.

The place of skill in the early years

Children aged 5–7 are flexible, agile and inquisitive. Through gymnastics activities, we want to channel these traits in the children so that they become skilful in managing their bodies in a variety of situations. Thus, the emphasis is on skilful control of the actions the child has chosen rather than mastery of gymnastics skills chosen by the teacher. The focus will be on the individual children's needs within the class, where there will be, inevitably, a wide ability range. This may mean that one child is still at the early stage of development whereas another is at the later developmental stage. Some children will be ready to focus on work that is more characteristically 'gymnastic', and this is where the 'Specific skills guide' (in the final section of this workbook, page 169) will be useful to teachers. In order to extend the children's capability, there are some specific skills included in the later sessions.

In their classes, teachers may have a few children who have been taught gymnastics skills at a club. These children may be very skilful in this respect, and teachers may be apprehensive about safety factors, or worry that other children may emulate them. This is why most of the content of the sessions in this workbook calls for individual, inventive responses (very different from the way gymnastics clubs operate). However, the more able children can often be a source of inspiration for others and, especially, will be able to share ideas and demonstrate good quality.

Teachers may have to explain this to the children who just want to perform their skills and, additionally, encourage them to be inventive by trying other ways of answering the set tasks. If teachers use the ideas outlined in the sessions, they will be able to broaden children's movement vocabulary and develop their performance capabilities.

Where tasks relate to teaching specific skills, reference should be made to the 'Specific skills guide' (page 169). For information on teaching further skills, see *Developing Physical Health and Well-being Through Gymnastics (7–11)*, as it is most important that this whole programme of gymnastics sessions is seen as a progressive learning package.

So what about assessment?

Assessment *for* learning and *of* learning should be integral to gymnastics sessions. Teachers will need to assess the children's physical competence and also the extent to which there is increasing development of their understanding of health, well-being and cross-curricular aspects of learning (concern for others, safety, giving and receiving feedback, and so on).

In addition to teacher assessment, the children should be encouraged to engage in self-assessment and peer-assessment. Examples of these will be found in the session plans that follow.

In the sessions, children will be trying out movements, thinking about them and then refining them. As such, they will need to learn about the kinds of criteria against which they will be able to assess themselves and others and, in doing so, begin to take responsibility for their own development and learning. The teacher can use different strategies to achieve this:

- modelling and demonstration of good practice;
- mini plenary sessions to reinforce expectations; and
- reviewing performances with focussed feedback.

Children should be encouraged to discuss and evaluate their work at the end of each session in preparation for the next. These opportunities can happen in the classroom after the lesson.

Judiciously planned use of ICT will also help the children and the teachers in this process as they record, observe and assess themselves in action.

The approach

In order to facilitate teachers' selection of session content and its presentation to the children, this workbook is written in a session-by-session format (called *the session plan*) for the two years of Key Stage 1.

The sessions can be adapted, developed or used for consolidation, dependent on the time and resources available and/or the children's ability levels.

The individual sessions are preceded by an *overall plan* that will give teachers an overview of the programme to be taught during each of the two years.

The overall plan

The overall plan sets out the focus, aspects for consolidation and learning objectives for each of the sessions in Years 1 and 2, and, in this way, shows the progression that has been built into the whole two-year programme.

This pattern should continue from Year 2 into Year 3 to support the transition process and avoid regression in the children's learning (see *Developing Physical Health and Well-being Through Gymnastics (7–11)*).

Inserted into the overall plan are pages specifically intended for teachers' ongoing comments and notes.

The session plan

The session plan is a detailed plan derived from the overall plan. It is an easy-to-follow guide for teachers and student teachers delivering the sessions. There are 40 session plans (20 for Year 1 and 20 for Year 2), which have:

- *a title* that forms the focus for the session;
- *learning objectives* relating to physical development, to aspects of general health and well-being and to aspects of broader learning across the curriculum; and
- *assessment criteria* that indicate the questions the teachers and the children should be asking themselves about what has been learned.

In most cases, consolidation from the previous session is built into the plan. *Sessions 1, 10 and 20, in both years, are for assessment purposes only.*

All sessions have warm-up, floor work and calming down activities. Most also have apparatus. There is encouragement for the teacher to discuss the children's work in the classroom after each session.

It is particularly important to use this time to help the children articulate their understanding of their performances and how to improve upon them. Additionally, discussion of health and well-being might best be focussed after the sessions, as well as after the session warm-up.

Warm-up

This should be vigorous so that the children have the opportunity to develop strength, speed, flexibility and stamina. Warm-ups can provide opportunities for children to consolidate skills and actions learned in previous sessions. They also enable teachers to incorporate activities that support children's learning about their personal well-being, as they are actively experiencing changes in how they are feeling (for example, breathing heavily when active).

Floor work

This centres upon the development of skills and actions. It provides opportunities for children to select and refine these skills and combine them in a sequence, working towards an ultimate performance. Within the sessions, through demonstration, observation, modelling, questioning and reflection, children will gain an understanding of the performance criteria, which will encourage them to take responsibility for their own learning and become independent learners. Through this, they will have opportunities to develop skills such as problem-solving, sharing ideas and giving feedback.

Apparatus work

This is used as an extension of floor work. In Year 1, children should be encouraged to continue to replicate skills developed on the floor and explore these skills on the apparatus. They will discover that they may have to adapt their movements on the apparatus. The teacher should encourage them to be constantly active to maximise the opportunity for development of stamina, strength, speed and flexibility.

In Year 2, children will use a more restricted floor space so that they can adapt sequences learned on the floor on to the apparatus, spending more time refining their performances.

Cool-down/calming down

This provides the opportunity for teachers to show children that they need to cool-down after physical activity, and also it prepares them for returning calmly to the classroom.

The content of the sessions varies so that there are:

- simple activities done together (including the teacher) to develop a corporate sense of belonging;
- challenges in which children, through exploration, try to find their own way of responding, working individually and discovering their own capabilities; and

- ideas from the teacher and from the children put forward to help the children create patterns of movements that can be repeated and performed (this will support their sequencing skills and their movement memories).

In Year 1, this conscious awareness of what the children are doing is exploited to increase their understanding and skill, together with learning about how the space around them can be used to good advantage.

Situations in which the children learn to use this knowledge, together with more control and skill, are developed further in Year 2, during which movements begin to be more characteristically 'gymnastic'.

Differentiation

Within the sessions, the teacher will need to ensure all the children have opportunities to engage and achieve. This is essential for individual progression, and is likely to take place at different rates. To support differentiation the teacher will consider, for example, how much input is given, length of sequences, and whether the children work individually or in pairs. In order to differentiate the work, the teacher may, for example, ask children to:

- add more or fewer actions to a sequence;
- work on their own or with a partner; or
- practise and perform selected skills independently, or with direction from the teacher.

Children should also be encouraged to work on the quality of their movement – for example:

- stretch/extend the feet and toes;
- hold the body tension; and
- add changes in direction, levels or speed to make the sequence more pleasing to an audience.

The assessment activities and assessment criteria

The use of assessment activities in particular sessions, in both years, will allow teachers to find out what the children can do, what they know and what they understand. They will then have knowledge of the individual so that they can build upon, extend and measure progress. The teachers can then use this information, as appropriate, as a reference point for the next session or sessions they teach. As it is difficult for teachers to monitor the whole class, it is important that varied resources are used, where appropriate, to support the monitoring process. For example, ICT in the form of a digital camera and a camcorder are ideal to record children's movements. Teaching assistants may also be asked to offer support in this respect.

Teachers may wish to consider the benefits of involving those children who are unable to participate in a session by having them take a focussed, evaluative role.

Children can learn to observe others' movements, and this will help their understanding, assist their language development and increase the range of activities they can do. This form of assessment is an integral part of all the sessions that follow.

All sessions should include opportunities for children to show their work (performance) individually, in pairs, in small groups or to the whole class (these could be in mini plenary periods in the middle and at the end of sessions, giving opportunities for ongoing feedback).

The place of demonstration and modelling

Built into the session plans are opportunities for children to see others' work to promote understanding of worthwhile performance. Demonstrations by individual children need to be purposeful. Half the class watching the rest can prove to be a non-productive use of precious time unless those observing are asked to look at an identified small group of children.

The teacher can select one child to show the rest how to perform a specific task that is about to be attempted, such as a bunny jump. Or, a child may be selected to show the others how he/she has responded to a task, demonstrating inventiveness/creativity, so that the other children can try this for themselves. Others may be chosen to show particularly good quality work – they will be modelling the quality to which the others may aspire.

In all instances, it is best to confirm with the child first that he/she is prepared to demonstrate, and all demonstrations should be followed up by a discussion with the children about what they have seen.

In certain circumstances, where the teacher has confidence, he/she may demonstrate a movement for the children to inform the improvement of their performance, or the accuracy of what they are trying to do.

There are examples of all these ideas in the sessions for both Year 1 and Year 2.

Apparatus

This workbook ideally requires the following apparatus for a class of 30 children to ensure maximum activity:

- 6 benches
- 4 planks
- 1 climbing frame
- 10 mats
- 3 stools/stacking tables
- 1 bar box
- 1 agility/movement table.

Organisation

It is the responsibility of the teacher to make sure that any children handling apparatus do so correctly and safely.

We have not included suggestions for the layout of apparatus, as children are capable of deciding where to place the pieces, under the guidance of the teacher. It *must*, however, be checked by the teacher before use.

The children should put out the apparatus in such a way that there is still space to explore movement on the floor around the apparatus. They will need to:

- learn to lift, carry and place apparatus safely;
- learn to work as a team assembling and dismantling apparatus;
- be grouped carefully to enable them to carry the apparatus together; and
- know where they are placing equipment – this can be helped by sitting the children in the area where the apparatus is to be placed.

Apparatus should be of a suitable height for the children, and this should be progressive as the children move from Year 1 to Year 2.

They should not jump down from a height higher than themselves and mats should be placed where children will be jumping from a piece of apparatus.

The apparatus should be stored at strategic positions around the sides of the room in readiness, so that all children have to do is lift it into position.

Handling the apparatus

Children need to be taught how to lift, carry and place equipment safely. A detailed session has been dedicated to this in Session 2 of Year 1, with follow-up sessions providing opportunities for further consolidation. By Year 2, the children should be proficient in moving apparatus, and so the session on handling the apparatus will serve as a reminder of good habits. The following should be noted:

- There should be four children to each heavy piece of equipment – two on each side. They should lift it together and put it down together.

- There should be four children to each mat – two on each side. Holding the mats on the corners should be avoided, as this can cause damage. Mats should be lifted and not dragged, and put away tidily.

- Children should always carry equipment while walking and, wherever possible, facing forwards.

- All hooks, Velcro® and bolts must be securely in position, and the teacher *must* check the apparatus assembly before children use it.

Safety

The safety of the children must be uppermost in the teacher's mind at all times, and in accordance with the local authority regulations. The Association for Physical Education (afPE) should also be a source of reference (*Safe Practice in Physical Education and School Sport – 2008*).

A general, agreed policy throughout the school will ensure safe and simple guidelines for every teacher.

Teachers should take inhalers (for children who require them) and first aid kits to every session.

The hall

This area in most Key Stage 1 settings is a multi-use space, and the following points need to be considered:

- The floor should be clean, splinter-proof and non-slippery.
- The working area should be clear of displays, workbook shelves, pianos, overhead projectors and so on, as these provide dangerous corners if a child accidentally bumps into them.

Clothing

The following points need to be considered regarding clothing:

- Children should change into appropriate clothing for a gymnastics session, such as shorts and a T-shirt.
- Where the floor is suitable, the children should work with bare feet.
- Jewellery should not be worn and long hair should be tied back.
- The teacher should also, of course, wear suitable clothing and safe footwear (bare feet, where the floor is suitable).

The teacher must be positioned where he/she can see the whole class at all times.

Overall plan
Year 1

Session 1

Assessment activity

This first session is for an initial assessment of the children's capabilities to ascertain what they know and what they can do.

INITIAL ASSESSMENT TASKS

Select two ways of travelling and link these in a short sequence.

Combine the actions with a clear body shape at the start of the sequence.

DISCUSSION

Ask the children what they know about changes to the body before, during and after activity.

ASSESSMENT CRITERIA – QUESTIONS TO CONSIDER

Physical

1   Can the children perform two travelling actions and combine them in a short sequence?

2   Can they add a starting shape, and remember and repeat their sequence with consistency, coordination and control (for example, arms and legs straight, toes and fingers stretched, body shapes held with good strong tension)?

Well-being

3   Can the children talk about changes in the body before, during and after exercise?

Broader learning

4   Can the children follow instructions effectively?

Session 2

Handling apparatus safely

Consolidation from previous session: travelling in different ways (running, jumping, hopping and skipping).

LEARNING OBJECTIVES

Physical

1 To know how to lift, carry and place apparatus safely.

2 To know that it is important to work as a team when lifting heavy equipment.

Well-being

3 To know how lifting, carrying and placing equipment safely is important to health and well-being.

Broader learning

4 To recognise and respond to issues of safety relating to themselves and others, and know how to get help.

Session 3

Starting and finishing positions

Consolidation from previous session: to combine actions in a sequence; to lift, carry and place the equipment safely.

LEARNING OBJECTIVES

Physical

1   To learn from each other a range of body shapes to start and finish their sequence.

2   To know what makes a good starting and finishing position.

Well-being

3   To know why activity is good for health and well-being.

Broader learning

4   To share ideas with a partner and give feedback in a positive manner.

Session 4

Going and stopping

Consolidation from previous session: to combine actions in a sequence with a starting and finishing position; to lift, carry and place equipment safely.

LEARNING OBJECTIVES

Physical

1   To be able to hold still positions within a sequence.

2   To be able to identify when the body is tense and when it is relaxed.

Well-being

3   To know about some of the benefits of activity to health and well-being.

Broader learning

4   To share ideas with a partner and give feedback.

Session 5

Slide and spin

Consolidation from previous session: to combine actions in a sequence, holding an action still with strong body tension to add interest to a performance; to lift, carry and place equipment safely.

LEARNING OBJECTIVES

Physical

1   To know which body parts can be used for sliding and spinning.

2   To be able to select sliding and spinning actions, and combine them with a change of direction.

Well-being

3   To continue to learn about the benefits of activity to health and well-being.

Broader learning

4   To identify strengths in a partner's performance.

For notes and comments

Session 6

Push and pull

Consolidation from previous session: to slide and spin on different body parts and add a change of direction; to lift, carry and place equipment safely.

LEARNING OBJECTIVES

Physical

1 To know how to use pushing or pulling when performing an action.

2 To know how to include a starting and finishing body shape in a sequence.

Well-being

3 To understand some changes that happen to bodies from birth and see how this relates to what skills they are now capable of.

Broader learning

4 To know how to give positive feedback and why this is important.

Session 7

Jumping and landing

Consolidation from previous session: to identify what body parts are used to push and pull; to add a starting and/or finishing body shape to sequences; to lift, carry and place equipment safely.

LEARNING OBJECTIVES

Physical

1   To know about and demonstrate different ways of jumping.

2   To combine two 'like' actions together in a sequence.

Well-being

3   To identify the new skills they have learned.

Broader learning

4   To give positive feedback and say why this is important.

Session 8

Hopping and skipping

Consolidation from previous session: to jump in two different ways and land with bent knees; to lift, carry and place equipment safely.

LEARNING OBJECTIVES

Physical

1   To know that adding a change of direction to body movements adds interest to a performance.

2   To know how to combine hopping and skipping actions.

Well-being

3   To be able to identify the benefits of being physically active.

Broader learning

4   To be able to praise others' performances and know why this is important.

Session 9

Rocking and rolling

Consolidation from previous session: to perform hopping and skipping actions in a sequence that includes a change of direction; to lift, carry and place equipment safely.

LEARNING OBJECTIVES

Physical

1   To make a sequence on the floor and apparatus.

2   To select different body parts on which to rock and roll.

Well-being

3   To identify changes that occur to their bodies when they are active, and how this contributes to their health and well-being.

Broader learning

4   To work as a team to lift, carry and place equipment safely.

Session 10

Assessment activity

This session is for interim assessment. It is intentionally very similar to the first assessment, in Session 1, so that the teacher can evaluate the children's progress. There is only floor work.

ASSESSMENT TASK

Select two ways of travelling and link these in a short sequence.

Combine the actions with a starting and finishing body shape/action.

DISCUSSION

Ask the children to identify the changes that happen to the body during activity, and the benefits of being active to their health and well-being.

ASSESSMENT CRITERIA – QUESTIONS TO CONSIDER

1   Can the children perform two travelling actions and combine them in a sequence?

2   Can they add a starting and finishing shape/action, and remember and repeat their sequence with consistency, coordination and control (for example, arms and legs straight, toes and fingers stretched, body shapes held with good strong tension)?

3   Do they know what changes happen to their bodies when they are active, and the benefits of being active to their health and well-being?

4   Can they follow instructions and solve problems (for example, select travelling actions and add to a sequence)?

For notes and comments

Session 11

Big and small

Consolidation from previous session: to rock and roll on different body parts and combine in a sequence; to describe another's actions; to lift, carry and place equipment safely.

LEARNING OBJECTIVES

Physical

1 To know that, by making themselves big, they take up more space and when small, less space.

2 To revise and learn a variety of stepping actions.

Well-being

3 To know about physical similarities and differences in others – and why this is important.

Broader learning

4 To move around without colliding, and to know why this is important.

Session 12

High and low

Consolidation from previous session: to explore big and small steps, lightly and heavily; to lift, carry and place equipment safely.

LEARNING OBJECTIVES

Physical

1   To be able to perform actions at different levels.

2   To be able to combine 'like' actions in a sequence.

Well-being

3   To know about physical similarities and differences in others – and why this is important.

Broader learning

4   To be able to talk about how their movements have improved.

Session 13

Wide and narrow

Consolidation from previous session: to perform actions at different levels; to lift, carry and place equipment safely.

LEARNING OBJECTIVES

Physical

1   To adapt movements on narrow and wide surfaces.

2   To remember and replicate a sequence.

Well-being

3   To know why being active is good for physical development.

Broader learning

4   To work as part of a team when getting out equipment.

Session 14

Being aware of body parts – touching the floor with different body parts

Consolidation from previous session: to perform actions with wide and narrow body shapes; to lift, carry and place equipment safely.

LEARNING OBJECTIVES

Physical

1   To identify light and heavy movements.

2   To remember a sequence of movements.

Well-being

3   To consciously name different body parts that are used during gymnastic activity.

Broader learning

4   To be able to solve movement problems independently.

Session 15

Being aware of body parts – travelling on hands and feet

Consolidation from previous session: to name body parts and select actions to refine, remember and perform in a sequence; to lift, carry and place equipment safely.

LEARNING OBJECTIVES

Physical

1 To learn to balance on hands and feet.

2 To know and demonstrate a range of ways of travelling on hands and feet.

Well-being

3 To practise and work independently.

Broader learning

4 To share and learn from others' ideas.

For notes and comments

Session 16

Travelling on different body parts

Consolidation from previous session: to take weight on hands and feet; to combine actions in a sequence; to lift, carry and place equipment safely.

LEARNING OBJECTIVES

Physical

1   To continue to learn to travel on different body parts.

2   To know how to hold, still and clearly, a starting position.

Well-being

3   To know about the changes that happen to the body when active.

Broader learning

4   To listen to and show consideration for others when watching their work.

Session 17

Keeping still while on hands and feet

Consolidation from previous session: to travel on different body parts; to add a starting position that can be held still at the beginning of a sequence; to lift, carry and place equipment safely.

LEARNING OBJECTIVES

Physical

1   To know when the body is tense and when it is relaxed.

2   To continue to learn to balance on hands and feet.

Well-being

3   To continue to develop an understanding of the changes that happen to the body during activity, and the benefits of this to physical health.

Broader learning

4   To work as a team to lift, carry and place equipment.

Session 18

Holding stretched and tucked positions

Consolidation from previous session: to take weight on hands and feet; to combine actions to form a sequence; to lift, carry and place equipment safely.

LEARNING OBJECTIVES

Physical

1   To know how to stretch and tuck the body, and hold good body tension.

2   To combine tucking and stretching actions in a sequence.

Well-being

3   To know and understand the importance of changing into the correct clothing for PE (with long hair tied back).

Broader learning

4   To work as a team to lift, carry and place equipment.

Session 19

Moving in extended and tucked positions

Consolidation from previous session: to know how to stretch and tuck the body; to combine actions to make a sequence; to lift, carry and place equipment safely.

LEARNING OBJECTIVES

Physical

1 To know when the body is stretched (extended) and when it is tucked.

2 To be able to give feedback to peers against set criteria.

Well-being

3 To reinforce the importance of changing into the correct clothing for PE.

Broader learning

4 To follow instructions in answer to movement problems.

Session 20

Final assessment activity

This session will assess children's knowledge and understanding gained from the sessions throughout the year. Children should be encouraged to take responsibility for their own learning by identifying what they can achieve, what they need to do to develop and how they will do this.

ASSESSMENT TASKS

On the floor

Select two 'like' ways of travelling on different body parts with contrasting body shapes (for example, jumping high and then low, wide and narrow, big and small, stretched and tucked). Link these in a short sequence and practise the sequence so it can be remembered and performed well.

Add a starting body shape and finishing shape, or action, to the sequence.

On the apparatus

Explore the apparatus, transferring the same actions from the floor on to the apparatus.

DISCUSSION

Talk about what changes happen to the body when it is active, and the benefits of being active to your health and well-being.

Describe the new skills that you have learned.

Discuss your work and say what you might do to make it even better.

ASSESSMENT CRITERIA – QUESTIONS TO CONSIDER

1 Can the children perform two travelling actions and combine them with contrasting body shapes in a sequence?

2 Can they add a starting shape and a finishing shape, or action?

3 Can they remember and perform the sequence with consistency, coordination and control?

4 Can they talk about the changes that happen to their bodies when they are active, and the benefits of being active to their health and well-being?

5 Can they talk about the new skills they have learned?

6 Can they identify actions/movements that they can perform well and know one or two ways in which they can improve?

For notes and comments

For notes and comments

Overall plan
Year 2

Session 1

Assessment activity

This session is intentionally similar to Session 20 from Year 1 so that the teacher can re-assess and reflect on the impact the summer break and transition into Year 2 has had on the children's progress. It is possible that growth spurts may also have impacted on their skill level. There is both floor and apparatus work.

ASSESSMENT TASKS

On the floor

Select two 'like' ways of travelling on different body parts with contrasting body shapes (for example, jumping high and then low, wide and narrow, big and small, stretched and tucked). Link these in a short sequence and practise the sequence so it can be remembered and performed well.

Add a starting body shape and finishing shape, or action, to the sequence.

On the apparatus

Explore the apparatus, transferring the same actions from the floor on to the apparatus.

DISCUSSION

Talk about what changes happen to the body when it is active, and the benefits of being active to your health and well-being.

Describe the new skills that you have learned.

Discuss your work and say what you might do to make it even better.

ASSESSMENT CRITERIA – QUESTIONS TO CONSIDER

1 Can the children perform two travelling actions and combine them with contrasting body shapes in a sequence?

2 Can they add a starting shape and a finishing shape, or action?

3 Can they remember and perform the sequence with consistency, coordination and control?

4 Can they talk about the changes that happen to their bodies when they are active, and the benefits of being active to their health and well-being?

5 Can they talk about the new skills they have learned?

6 Can they identify actions/movements that they can perform well and know one or two ways in which they can improve?

Session 2

Handling apparatus safely

This session is to reinforce Session 2 from Year 1 ('Handling apparatus safely') so that the children are clear about the expectations for Year 2 (which should be progressive in terms of the children taking more responsibility).

LEARNING OBJECTIVES

Physical

1   To know how to lift, carry and place apparatus safely.

2   To know that it is important to work as a team when lifting heavy equipment.

Well-being

3   To know why lifting, carrying and placing equipment safely is important to health and well-being.

Broader learning

4   To recognise and respond to issues of safety relating to themselves and others, and know how to get help.

Session 3

Slide, spin, push, pull

Consolidation from previous session: to lift, carry and place equipment safely.

LEARNING OBJECTIVES

Physical

1   To know how to perform sliding and spinning actions using the body to push and pull.

2   To recognise the differences when some actions are performed at different levels.

Well-being

3   To identify physical changes to the body during activity.

Broader learning

4   To be able to listen and respond to their peers in a positive manner.

Session 4

Jumping, hopping and skipping

Consolidation from previous session: to slide, spin, push and pull, and link two or more actions together; to lift, carry and place equipment safely.

LEARNING OBJECTIVES

Physical

1 To be able to replicate actions in a sequence.

2 To develop an awareness of ways to make sequences more interesting to an audience.

Well-being

3 To identify the new skills they have learned.

Broader learning

4 To know some of the strengths in their work and be able to identify ways that will help them improve.

Session 5

Using actions with rotation (turning)

Consolidation from previous session: to combine jumping, hopping and skipping actions in a sequence; to adapt movements on to the apparatus; to lift, carry and place equipment safely.

LEARNING OBJECTIVES

Physical

1   To be able to replicate a sequence of actions.

2   To understand the terms 'rotate' and 'spin'.

Well-being

3   To know that healthy eating and physical activity are beneficial to health and well-being.

Broader learning

4   To know how attitude and behaviour may impact on others.

For notes and comments

Session 6

Travelling quickly or slowly

Consolidation from previous session: to rotate the body by spinning and turning at different levels; to lift, carry and place equipment safely.

LEARNING OBJECTIVES

Physical

1   To be able to demonstrate the term 'gradual' as the speed quickens and slows in sequences.

2   To be able to discuss the criteria for holding good body control.

Well-being

3   To know why it is important to change clothing to be ready for physical activity.

Broader learning

4   To know the importance of moving safely around the hall and on apparatus.

Session 7

Strongly and lightly

Consolidation from previous session: to perform movements with varied speeds; to lift, carry and place equipment safely.

LEARNING OBJECTIVES

Physical

1   To know that movements and actions can be performed strongly and lightly.

2   To be able to share movement ideas with a partner.

Well-being

3   To identify how the body feels during and after activity.

Broader learning

4   To know what has to be done to improve a performance.

Session 8

Moving in different directions

Consolidation from previous session: to perform movements and/or actions either in a light or strong manner; to lift, carry and place equipment safely.

LEARNING OBJECTIVES

Physical

1   To know the different directional terms (forwards, backwards, sideways and diagonally), and be able to apply these to actions.

2   To be able to remember and perform a sequence.

Well-being

3   To know that healthy eating and physical activity are beneficial to health and well-being.

Broader learning

4   To know how to give supportive feedback to a partner after a performance.

Session 9

Moving up, down and sideways

Consolidation from previous session: to travel in different directions (forwards, sideways, backwards and diagonally); to lift, carry and place equipment safely.

LEARNING OBJECTIVES

Physical

1   To know that movements can be performed both at different levels and in different directions.

2   To be able to work with a partner to produce a sequence that can be remembered and performed.

Well-being

3   To know that healthy eating and physical activity are beneficial to health and well-being.

Broader learning

4   To identify strengths and know how to improve.

Session 10

Assessment activity

This session is for interim assessment. It assesses what children have learned in previous sessions so that the teacher can evaluate their progress and determine what needs to be reinforced in the next sessions. There is only floor work.

ASSESSMENT TASKS

On the floor

Combine three travelling actions that include one or more of the following: a change of speed/direction/level. Combine these actions with a starting body shape and finish with a rotation.

Practise, remember and perform the sequence.

DISCUSSION

Talk about what changes happen to the body when it is active, and the benefits of being active to your health and well-being.

Discuss your work and say what you might do to make it even better.

ASSESSMENT CRITERIA – QUESTIONS TO CONSIDER

1   Can the children perform three travelling actions in a sequence, showing a change of direction/speed/level?

2   Can they add a starting shape and a rotation movement to complete their sequence?

3 Can they remember and perform the sequence with consistency, coordination and control?

4 Can they talk about the changes that happen to their bodies when they are active, and the benefits of being active to their health and well-being?

5 Can they talk about the new skills they have learned?

6 Can they identify actions/movements that they can perform well, and know one or two ways in which they can improve?

For notes and comments

Taking weight/holding still positions

Consolidation from previous session: to perform actions by springing high and low, and moving sideways; to lift, carry and place equipment safely.

LEARNING OBJECTIVES

Physical

1   To demonstrate different balances on feet and hands.

2   To know how to balance on the apparatus in a variety of ways.

Well-being

3   To know that being active is good for health and well-being.

Broader learning

4   To know that, when working with a partner, it is important to share ideas.

Session 12

Transferring weight from feet to hands (1)

Consolidation from previous session: to take weight on feet and hands in different combinations while still; to lift, carry and place equipment safely.

LEARNING OBJECTIVES

Physical

1   To know how to take weight on hands and feet in a variety of ways.

2   To know what is meant by 'distributing weight'.

Well-being

3   To be aware that some substances are harmful to the body.

Broader learning

4   To know how to share ideas with one another, and know why it is important to be able to do so.

Session 13

Transferring weight from feet to hands (2)

Consolidation from previous session: to perform bunny hops (forwards, sideways, backwards and diagonally); to lift, carry and place equipment safely.

LEARNING OBJECTIVES

Physical

1 To know how to take weight on hands and feet to form a cartwheel shape.

2 To know how to transfer weight from one hand to another on apparatus.

Well-being

3 To know that other factors contribute to health and well-being in addition to being active.

Broader learning

4 To identify what they do well and what they have to do to improve.

Session 14

Transferring body weight

Consolidation from previous session: to perform bunny hops and transfer weight from hand to hand to form a cartwheel shape; to lift, carry and place equipment safely.

LEARNING OBJECTIVES

Physical

1   To know how to balance on different body parts.

2   To be able to devise a sequence that can be remembered.

Well-being

3   To be able to identify how the body feels after being active.

Broader learning

4   To listen to and show consideration for the views of a partner.

Session 15

Jumping and landing with feet either together or apart

Consolidation from previous session: to move from one balance into another; to lift, carry and place equipment safely.

LEARNING OBJECTIVES

Physical

1   To develop the control and coordination of gymnastics movements.

2   To improve performance by observation.

Well-being

3   To recognise how it feels to receive feedback from others.

Broader learning

4   To identify the help required in order to develop floor work and apparatus work.

For notes and comments

Session 16

Travelling on hands and feet, with feet either together or apart

Consolidation from previous session: to jump with feet apart or together; to lift, carry and place equipment safely.

LEARNING OBJECTIVES

Physical

1 To improve a performance using particular criteria for the evaluation.

2 To devise a sequence with a partner.

Well-being

3 To identify the new skills they have learned.

Broader learning

4 To identify their own and others' strengths.

Session 17

Sliding and rolling, with feet either together or apart

Consolidation from previous session: to travel with feet together or apart; to lift, carry and place equipment safely.

LEARNING OBJECTIVES

Physical

1   To develop skills of rolling and sliding.

2   To use criteria and observation to develop the rolls.

Well-being

3   To know that a healthy diet is important for health and well-being.

Broader learning

4   To know how to perform actions safely, and with consideration for others.

Session 18

Travelling along straight lines

Consolidation from previous session: to slide and roll sideways, with feet apart and together; to lift, carry and place equipment safely.

LEARNING OBJECTIVES

Physical

1   To be able to control and coordinate actions while moving in a straight line.

2   To use criteria and observation to develop sequences.

Well-being

3   To know clearly some of the benefits of physical activity to health and well-being.

Broader learning

4   To negotiate and collaborate in order to devise a sequence of movements.

Session 19

Travelling using zigzag pathways

Consolidation from previous session: to travel in a straight line in a variety of ways; to lift, carry and place equipment safely.

LEARNING OBJECTIVES

Physical

1 To be able to control and coordinate actions using a zigzag pathway.

2 To use criteria and observation to develop sequences.

Well-being

3 To identify what is good in a partner's performance and share this together.

Broader learning

4 To work with another person cooperatively.

Session 20

Assessment activity

This session has the final assessment tasks for Key Stage 1.

It assesses what children have learned across both Year 1 and Year 2.

Teachers should identify the stage of development at which each child is consistently working (early, middle or later) so that this information can be transferred to Year 3, and the children can continue to build on what they have already learned.

This session includes both floor and apparatus work.

ASSESSMENT TASKS

On the floor

Combine three travelling actions that include one or more of the following: a change of speed/direction/level.

Add to this by including a starting body shape and a finishing movement.

Practise, remember and perform the sequence.

On the apparatus

Transfer your travelling actions/movements from the floor on to the apparatus (for example, start on the floor, move towards the apparatus and then either travel on to, along, over or off, using one or more of your movements). Finish with a rotation action.

DISCUSSION

Explain what you must do to stay healthy and well.

Talk about what is good work and say what you might do to make it even better.

ASSESSMENT CRITERIA – QUESTIONS TO CONSIDER

1   Can the children perform three travelling actions in a sequence showing a change of direction/speed/level?

2   Can they add a starting shape and a rotation movement to complete their sequence?

3   Can they remember and perform the sequence with consistency, coordination and control?

4   Can they talk about the changes that happen to their bodies when they are active, and the benefits of being active to their health and well-being?

5   Can they identify actions/movements that they can perform well, and know one or two ways in which they can improve?

For notes and comments

For notes and comments

The sessions

Year 1

SESSION 1

Assessment activity

This first session is for an initial assessment of the children's capabilities to ascertain what they know and what they can do.

INITIAL ASSESSMENT TASKS

Select two ways of travelling and link these in a short sequence.

Combine the actions with a clear body shape at the start of the sequence.

DISCUSSION

Ask the children what they know about changes to the body before, during and after activity.

ASSESSMENT CRITERIA – QUESTIONS TO CONSIDER

Physical

1   Can the children perform two travelling actions and combine them in a short sequence?

2   Can they add a starting shape, and remember and repeat their sequence with consistency, coordination and control (for example, arms and legs straight, toes and fingers stretched, body shapes held with good strong tension)?

Well-being

3   Can the children talk about changes in the body before, during and after exercise?

Broader learning

4   Can the children follow instructions effectively?

OUTCOME

Some children will achieve, some will excel and some will achieve less.

Warm-up

	Content	Teaching points
1	Run in and out of each other using all the hall space.	Keep your head up and eyes focussed on where you are going.
2	Do bouncy jumps in and out of each other.	Bend knees slightly on take off and landing.
3	Skip high enough so your head reaches towards the ceiling.	Raise arms up to help lift centre of gravity so you can skip higher.
4	Play the 'Computer Game'. [*Children explore travelling actions, share ideas and respond to instructions (fast forward, pause and rewind.*]	Make sure children look over their shoulders when travelling backwards (to avoid collisions) and know why this is important.

Floor work

	Content	Teaching points
1	Find a way to travel around the hall close to the ground.	Verbalise children's responses (for example, 'Adam is sliding on his tummy' or 'Petra is taking her weight on her hands and feet').
2	Find another way of travelling.	The children should show different travelling actions. The teacher should verbalise their actions.
3	Choose a travelling action and, when I strike the tambour, change your travelling movement.	The class should watch one or two good examples (draw attention to change of actions, good body tension, stretched toes and fingers, and interesting body shapes).
4	Try this again.	Opportunity for assessment.
5	Practise these movements so you remember them.	The children should keep strong bodies and stretch their fingers and toes.
6	Find an in interesting body shape to start your movement pattern.	Share the children's responses and select two or three children to demonstrate.
7	Get into your starting positions and, on 'go', see if you can remember the two travelling actions you were practising. You decide when you change from one to the other.	Watch one or two performances (draw attention to creative body shapes, good body tension and changes from one movement to another).
8	Practise your sequence so you can remember it.	Draw attention to starting and refining. Share some examples.
	ASSESSMENT – By the teacher (in conjunction with a teaching assistant where applicable), and also peer assessment by the children. Use ICT to record as many performances as possible so the children can self-assess during the lesson and in the classroom. This can also be kept as a record of their achievement.	

Cool-down/calming down

Walk around the room, stretch up high and curl up tightly. Wait until you are tapped and then line up. [*Enrol some children to help.*]

Classroom

Identify what the children thought they had done well and what they need to do to improve for the next lesson.

SESSION 2
Handling apparatus safely

Consolidation from previous session: travelling in different ways (running, jumping, hopping and skipping).

LEARNING OBJECTIVES

The objectives of the session need to be made explicit to the children. They also need to assess the extent to which they have achieved them.

Physical

1   To know how to lift, carry and place apparatus safely.

2   To know that it is important to work as a team when lifting heavy equipment.

Well-being

3   To know how lifting, carrying and placing equipment safely is important to health and well-being.

Broader learning

4   To recognise and respond to issues of safety relating to themselves and others, and know how to get help.

ASSESSMENT CRITERIA – QUESTIONS TO CONSIDER

1   Can the children follow the teacher's and the leader's instructions when they lift, carry and place equipment?

2   Can they work as a team when they are lifting, carrying and placing equipment?

3   Do they know why they have to be careful when lifting, moving and placing equipment?

4   Are they clear that they should not get on any equipment until checked by the teacher, and do they know that they should ask the teacher for help if and when required?

Warm-up

	Content	Teaching points
1	Run, jump, hop and skip in and out of each other.	Get the muscles warm and prepare them to lift, carry and place equipment.
2	Run in and out of each other and get into groups of two, then six, and then four, when the instruction is given.	The children should organise themselves in the correct number. When in groups of four, the children should sit down in their group.

Apparatus organisation

	Content	Teaching points
1	Sit with your legs crossed and with straight backs. Whoever is doing this well will be the 'leader'.	Select children to demonstrate straight backs and ask the children when it is important to keep their backs straight (relate this to lifting). Select a leader.
2	You will now learn to lift a bench safely.	Select one group to demonstrate. Two children should stand on each side of the bench, opposite one another. When the leader says 'lift', all the children should lift together, with their legs slightly bent and backs straight. When the leader says 'carry', the children should walk forwards towards where the group was sitting and, when the leader says 'down', the children should place the bench on the floor.
3	Collect a bench with your group.	The teacher should highlight where groups are working as a team. All lifting, moving and placing should be by instruction from the leader. Once done, encourage the children to hold a balance on the floor (to accommodate different completion times).
4	Collect a mat with your group.	Two children should stand on each side of the mat, opposite each other – not on the corners. The teacher should highlight where groups are working as a team. All lifting, moving and placing should be by instruction from the leader. Again, when done, encourage the children to hold individual balances (to accommodate different completion times).
5	Collect another piece of equipment with your group. [*Depending on what's available, for example a bar box, a trestle table, an agility plank or slide ladders.*]	The groups should demonstrate the lifting, moving and placing of different equipment to the rest of the class. Highlight straight backs, slightly bent knees, and that all lifting, moving and placing should be by instruction from the leader while working as a team.
6	One group will get out the wall frame and demonstrate to the rest of the class.	Select a group to get out the wall frame and demonstrate to the rest of the class. Highlight the importance of securing bolts, ladders and so on.
7	Depending on individual equipment available, you will also need to show how to attach the various apparatus using Velcro®, bolts and hooks. Inform the children that equipment must be checked by the teacher before they climb on to any of it. Try to angle the equipment to make it more interesting.	

Apparatus

	Content	Teaching points
1	Use the floor space to travel either by running, jumping, hopping or skipping, and when you come to the apparatus, explore travelling movements (on to, along, over, across and off).	Verbalise the responses and select some children to show their ideas.
2	Return to your group and, on instruction from your leader, return equipment back to its original place.	

Cool-down/calming down

Find a space and make yourself as small as you can. On the count of six, gradually unfold your body and stretch as high or as wide as possible. Hold yourself fully stretched and then slowly return to your original position.

Classroom

Identify what the children thought they did well and what they need to do to improve for the next lesson.

'Two children along each side, opposite each other, but not at the corners.'

'Sit with your legs crossed and with straight backs.'

'Encourage the children to share what they liked about each other's shapes.'

'Explore the sequences on the floor, mats and apparatus (across, between, over, under, along, up and through).'

SESSION 3
Starting and finishing positions

Consolidation from previous session: to combine actions in a sequence; to lift, carry and place equipment safely.

LEARNING OBJECTIVES

The objectives of the session need to be made explicit to the children. They also need to assess the extent to which they have achieved them.

Physical

1   To learn, from each other, a range of body shapes to start and finish a sequence.

2   To know what makes a good starting and finishing position.

Well-being

3   To know why activity is good for health and well-being.

Broader learning

4   To share ideas with a partner and give feedback in a positive manner.

ASSESSMENT CRITERIA – QUESTIONS TO CONSIDER

1   Can the children learn, from each other, a range of body shapes to start and finish their sequence?

2   Do they know what makes a good starting and finishing position?

3   Can they talk about why activity is good for them?

4   Can they share ideas with a partner and give feedback in a positive manner?

Warm-up

	Content	Teaching points
1	Run in and out of each other using all the hall space.	As in previous sessions.
2	With two feet together, do light bouncy jumps.	Place emphasis on springing *up*.
3	Do three springy jumps, stop and change direction, and then do three more.	The children should count to three when they stop, before changing direction and jumping again.
4	Do three springy jumps and then change level, making your jumps low and close to the floor.	The children should bend their knees and use their arms to balance.
5	Move around the hall, jumping. When the teacher claps, either change direction or your level.	Identify the children who are changing direction well, to reinforce this.

Floor work

1	Find an interesting shape that you could add to your jumping sequence.	Select two or three examples for the children to show, and involve the children in identifying why starting shapes are good/pleasing (for example, they can be held still, make interesting shapes and show good body tension).
2	Find another interesting shape and show it to a partner.	Encourage the children to share what they liked about each other's shapes.
3	Try out two different starting positions and select the one you like best. Practise it so that you have toes and fingers stretched and strong bodies held still.	Move around the hall, giving individual feedback and criteria to support good work.
4	Now combine your selected starting position with three jumps.	Draw attention to good body tension, stretched toes and fingers and slightly bent knees on take-off and landing.
5	Practise your sequence and add a finishing position.	Select a group of children to demonstrate and ask the other children to focus on one child, ready to give feedback on what they have noticed. Repeat as appropriate.

Apparatus

1	Hold a starting position and explore your jumping actions on the floor and apparatus (across, between, over, under, along and through).	Highlight well performed starting and finishing actions on the apparatus. Select individual children to show.
2	Find places on the apparatus to try out starting and finishing actions.	Encourage the children to try out some of their ideas from their floor work on the apparatus.

Cool-down/calming down

Find a space and imagine you are a spiky piece of ice – the sun comes out and you melt down into the ground.

Classroom

Identify what the children thought they did well and what they need to do to improve for the next lesson.

SESSION 4

Going and stopping

Consolidation from previous session: to combine actions in a sequence with a starting and finishing position; to lift, carry and place equipment safely.

LEARNING OBJECTIVES

The objectives of the session need to be made explicit to the children. They also need to assess the extent to which they have achieved them.

Physical

1   To be able to hold still positions within a sequence.
2   To be able to identify when the body is tense and when it is relaxed.

Well-being

3   To know about some of the benefits of activity to health and well-being.

Broader learning

4   To share ideas with a partner and give feedback.

ASSESSMENT CRITERIA – QUESTIONS TO CONSIDER

1   Can the children hold still positions within a sequence?
2   Can they control their bodies so that they can stop, tense and relax muscles – and recognise that they are doing this?
3   Can they identify why activity is good for them?
4   Can they share ideas with a partner and give positive feedback?

Warm-up

	Content	Teaching points
1	Explore travelling movements and, on the sound of one strike of the tambour, stop.	As you strike the tambour, say 'and stop'.
2	On two strikes of the tambour, hold your body shape still and tense your muscles.	The children should tense all those muscles so the body is rigid, so, if pushed, they would remain in that shape.
3	On three strikes of the tambour, relax your muscles.	The children should make all of their muscles floppy/go limp.
4	On four strikes of the tambour, find another way of travelling on a different part of your body.	Identify the range of response being shown.

Floor work

1	Remember one of the starting body shapes selected in the last lesson and try it again, or copy someone else's.	Verbalise interesting starting positions (for example, 'Sam is crouched up tight in a low position, ready to spring into his travelling action, giving a dramatic start to his performance').
2	Add a travelling action (run, skip, jump or hop) to it, and, on the sound of the tambour, hold your body still for the count of three.	Highlight good body tension and still shapes.
3	Find a partner (name yourselves 1 and 2). 1 should hold their starting position and then move into travelling actions. On the sound of the tambour, hold still for the count of three. Change over.	Peer assessment – each partner should identify when the body has good tension and is well held.

Apparatus

1	Explore the sequences on the floor, mats and apparatus (across, between, over, under, along, up and through).	Encourage the children to count up to three in their heads. Show good examples.
2	Find places on the apparatus where you can hold your shape still for the count of three.	The children should show strong body tension.

Cool-down/calming down

Hold a tense body shape, slowly relax your body and 'dissolve into the floor'.

Classroom

Identify what the children thought they did well and what they need to do to improve for the next lesson.

SESSION 5

Slide and spin

Consolidation from previous session: to combine actions in a sequence, holding an action still with strong body tension to add interest to a performance; to lift, carry and place equipment safely.

LEARNING OBJECTIVES

The objectives of the session need to be made explicit to the children. They also need to assess the extent to which they have achieved them.

Physical

1   To know which body parts can be used for sliding and spinning.

2   To be able to select sliding and spinning actions, and combine them with a change of direction.

Well-being

3   To continue to learn about the benefits of activity to health and well-being.

Broader learning

4   To identify strengths in a partner's performance.

ASSESSMENT CRITERIA – QUESTIONS TO CONSIDER

1   Can the children perform a range of sliding and spinning actions?

2   Can they combine these with a change of direction?

3   Can they explain why activity is important?

4   Can they talk about the strengths of a partner's performance?

Warm-up

	Content	Teaching points
1	Run in and out of each other, and, on the sound of the tambour, stop and change direction.	Select some children to show and articulate when and how they are changing direction.
2	Skip in and out of each other, and, on the sound of the tambour, stop and change direction.	Select some children to show and articulate when and how they are changing direction.
3	Jump (high, long, light and heavy) in and out of each other, and, on the sound of the tambour, stop and change direction.	Emphasise bending knees on take-off and landing.
4	Hop in and out of each other, and, on the sound of the tambour, stop and change direction.	The children should think about body tension.

Floor work

	Content	Teaching points
1	Find ways of sliding on different parts of your body (back, tummy, side, bottom and so on).	What other body parts are the children using to help them slide? Articulate responses and remind the children about body tension. Watch and share good examples.
2	Find another way to slide on your body.	This might include spins. Articulate responses so that ideas are shared with the whole class.
3	Find a way of spinning around. Now go back in the other direction.	Be mindful of spacing. Keep this activity short and articulate responses.
4	Select a way of sliding and, on the sound of the tambour, change to a spin.	Talk about how the children might do this as they experiment (for example, 'slide, slide, slide (tambour), spin and hold').
5	Find a partner and show each other your sequence.	Some children may be able to add a starting position. The children should tell their partner what they like about their sequence.

Apparatus

	Content	Teaching points
1	Find places where you can slide and spin on the floor, and on the apparatus (across, between, over, under, along and through).	Circulate and comment on what you see (for example, 'Mary is sliding on her tummy along the bench, and then spinning on the floor on her bottom').

Cool-down/calming down

Play 'Dead Fish' – lie still on the floor and, when you move, you have to form a seated line by the door. Who can be the last?

Classroom

Identify what the children thought they did well and what they need to do to improve for the next lesson.

SESSION 6

Push and pull

Consolidation from previous session: to slide and spin on different body parts and add a change of direction; to lift, carry and place equipment safely.

LEARNING OBJECTIVES

The objectives of the session need to be made explicit to the children. They also need to assess the extent to which they have achieved them.

Physical

1   To know how to use pushing or pulling when performing an action.

2   To know how to include a starting and finishing body shape in a sequence.

Well-being

3   To understand some changes that happen to bodies from birth and see how this relates to the skills they are now capable of.

Broader learning

4   To know how to give positive feedback and why this is important.

ASSESSMENT CRITERIA – QUESTIONS TO CONSIDER

1   Can the children identify which body parts they are using to 'pull' and 'push'?

2   Are they able to add a starting shape to a pushing and pulling action, and finish with a spin?

3   Can they talk about changes that have happened to their bodies since birth in relation to the skills they are now capable of?

4   Do they know how to give positive feedback and why this is important?

Warm-up

	Content	Teaching points
1	Explore a range of sliding and spinning actions. When the tambour sounds, on one strike, change direction (forwards, backwards, sideways or diagonally).	Select one or two children to show and highlight good body tension, stretched toes and fingers, and so on.
2	When the tambour sounds, on two strikes, change action.	Encourage the children to explore a range of actions. Select one or two children to show the class and identify interesting shapes within their work.
3	When the tambour sounds, on three strikes, hold your body shape still.	Draw attention to good posture.

Floor work

	Content	Teaching points
1	Explore ways of travelling around the floor on your back or tummy, using your feet and/or hands to push you.	Articulate the responses (for example, 'Sam is travelling on his back, using his feet to push himself'. Two or three children should demonstrate to the class. The class should identify whether the children are pushing or pulling.
2	Explore ways of travelling around the floor on your back or tummy, using your feet and/or hands to pull you around the hall.	Articulate the responses (for example, 'Sam is travelling on his back, using his feet to pull himself'. Two or three children should demonstrate to the class. The class should identify whether the children are pushing or pulling.
3	Choose how to push or pull yourself along.	On the sound of the tambour, the children should change their action. Remind them to keep good body tension.
4	Hold a starting position. Now travel on your back or tummy, and, on the sound of the tambour, add a spin.	The children should hold their starting position for the count of three, change and move for the count of three, and then spin. Encourage them to count to three in their head.
5	Practise on your own and see if you can remember your sequence. Practise and then, in pairs, show each other.	The children should each show their partner and then tell them what they are doing well.

Apparatus

	Content	Teaching points
1	Explore pushing and pulling actions on the floor, and find ways you can slide on the apparatus.	Circulate and question the children about which body parts they are using to push or pull themselves along.
2	Find places where you can spin on the apparatus.	Select children to show different actions on the apparatus. Ask the class to watch carefully and describe what they have seen.

Cool-down/calming down
Sit on the floor, spin around once, and then lie down quietly.

Classroom
Identify what the children thought they did well and what they need to do to improve for the next lesson.

SESSION 7

Jumping and landing

Consolidation from previous session: to identify what body parts are used to push and pull; to add a starting and/or finishing body shape to sequences; to lift, carry and place equipment safely.

LEARNING OBJECTIVES

The objectives of the session need to be made explicit to the children. They also need to assess the extent to which they have achieved them.

Physical

1   To know about and demonstrate different ways of jumping.

2   To combine two 'like' actions together in a sequence.

Well-being

3   To identify the new skills they have learned.

Broader learning

4   To give positive feedback and say why this is important.

ASSESSMENT CRITERIA – QUESTIONS TO CONSIDER

1   Can the children jump in different ways and combine these in a sequence?

2   Can they identify a way in which to develop their jumping action?

3   Can they identify the new skills they have learned?

4   Can they give positive feedback and say why this is important?

Warm-up

	Content	Teaching points
1	Find a way of travelling on your back or your tummy.	Encourage the children to identify whether they are pushing or pulling, and the body part they are using to do so (for example, 'James is using his legs to push himself along on his back on the floor').
2	Now do this again and change your direction.	Ask the children whether they have changed their action from a push to a pull, or vice versa. Choose children to demonstrate and encourage the class to describe the action.
3	Find a different body part to travel on and, when I clap my hands, change direction.	Select two or three examples to show and ask the children to watch. Select some children to describe the actions.

Floor work

	Content	Teaching points
1	Do little bouncy jumps anywhere in the hall.	Encourage the children to keep their feet together, and to bend their knees slightly on take-off and landing (resilient jumps like a bouncing ball) (see 'Specific skills guide', page 169).
2	Bend your knees and spring high into the air, and bend your knees on landing.	The emphasis is on the spring *up*. The children should use their arms to give them more lift.
3	Choose whether to do little bouncy jumps or high springy jumps. When I clap my hands, change your jump.	Highlight good examples (for example, 'Hari is changing his jumping action from a light bouncy jump to a high springy jump').
4	Hold a starting shape and then do three bouncy jumps and three high springy jumps. Try it again.	Select children to demonstrate. Ask the class, 'Where did he/she do a high springy jump?' Stress the difference between the two kinds of jumps.
5	With a partner, show each other your sequence. Tell your partner what you are trying to do to improve your jumping action.	Circulate to assess individual children and give formative feedback.

Apparatus

	Content	Teaching points
1	Use the floor space to explore little bouncy jumps and big springy jumps, and, when you come to the apparatus, explore jumping on to, along, over and off.	Circulate and comment on what you see (for example, 'Aisha is jumping on to and along the bench, jumping off and then landing with bent knees').

Cool-down/calming down

All play 'Jack in the Box' together. Start in a crouched position. All say, 'Jack in the Box jumps up like . . . *this*'. On the word 'this', do a big springy jump and then land in a crouched position.

Classroom

Identify what the children thought they did well and what they need to do to improve for the next lesson.

SESSION 8

Hopping and skipping

Consolidation from previous session: to jump in two different ways and land with bent knees; to lift, carry and place equipment safely.

LEARNING OBJECTIVES

The objectives of the session need to be made explicit to the children. They also need to assess the extent to which they have achieved them.

Physical

1   To know that adding a change of direction to body movements adds interest to a performance.
2   To know how to combine hopping and skipping actions.

Well-being

3   To be able to identify the benefits of being physically active.

Broader learning

4   To be able to praise others' performances and know why this is important.

ASSESSMENT CRITERIA – QUESTIONS TO CONSIDER

1   Can the children perform their actions and incorporate a change in direction?
2   Can they combine one or more actions together to make a sequence?
3   Can they talk about the benefits of being physically active?
4   Can they praise each others' performances and know why this is important?

Warm-up

	Content	Teaching points
1	Find a way of travelling in and out of each other on your feet. When I clap my hands, change your direction of travel (for example, to either backwards, sideways, or diagonal travel).	Verbalise the children's choices so ideas are shared. Select one or two children to demonstrate different directional movements.
2	Remember the two different jumping actions from the last session – light bouncy jumps and high springy jumps. Explore the space and, when I clap my hands, change from one jump to the other.	Select the children who remembered the last session to demonstrate, and highlight little bouncy jumps and high springy jumps.
3	Jump around the room and, when I clap my hands once, change your jumping action. When I clap my hands twice, change direction.	Select some children to demonstrate, and encourage the rest of the class to describe what is good about the sequences (for example, feet together, light quick bounces, bent knees on take-off and landing, arms used to lift and so on).

Floor work

	Content	Teaching points
1	Hop in and out of each other around the hall.	Encourage the children to travel forwards, backwards, sideways, holding a free foot, turning around and so on. Select a few examples for the class to watch. Highlight the use of arms and knees to gain height.
2	Skip in and out of each other. Now find different ways of skipping (low, high, backwards and so on).	Select some children to show their ideas.
3	Make up a movement pattern to include hopping and skipping actions. Practise so that you remember your pattern.	Ask the children whether they could change the order of their sequence to make it more interesting (for example, skip, hop, skip). Circulate to give formative feedback and assess whether the children know what they have to do to develop their movement patterns.
4	Show your sequences.	Select a group of children to show their sequences individually, and then repeat so that they all have a chance to show their sequences. The children should identify what they like about each other's performances. You should draw attention to good body tension, stretched fingers/toes and change of direction, and how these add interest to the performance.

Apparatus

	Content	Teaching points
1	Use the floor space to explore little bouncy jumps and big springy jumps and hopping and skipping actions. When you come to the apparatus, find places where you can jump, hop and skip on to, along, over and off.	Circulate and comment on what you see (for example, 'Mary is skipping up to the apparatus, hopping along the bench and jumping off the stool, landing with bent knees').

Cool-down/calming down
All play 'Jack in the Box' together. Start in a crouched position. All say, 'Jack in the Box jumps up like . . . *this*'. On the word 'this', do a big springy jump and then land in a crouched position.

Classroom
Identify what the children thought they did well and what they need to do to improve for the next lesson.

SESSION 9
Rocking and rolling

Consolidation from previous session: to perform hopping and skipping actions in a sequence that includes a change of direction; to lift, carry and place equipment safely.

LEARNING OBJECTIVES

The objectives of the session need to be made explicit to the children. They also need to assess the extent to which they have achieved them.

Physical

1   To make a sequence on the floor and apparatus.
2   To select different body parts on which to rock and roll.

Well-being

3   To identify changes that occur to their bodies when they are active and how this contributes to health and well-being.

Broader learning

4   To work as a team to lift, carry and place equipment safely.

ASSESSMENT CRITERIA – QUESTIONS TO CONSIDER

1   Can the children make a sequence on the floor and apparatus?
2   Are they able to select different body parts on which to rock and roll?
3   Can they identify changes that occur to their bodies when they are active and how this contributes to health and well-being?
4   Can they work as a team to lift, carry and place equipment safely?

Warm-up

	Content	Teaching points
1	Remember what you did last session and what you had to do to improve, and now practise these ideas.	Share some of the children's responses.
2	Move in and out of each other around the hall using jumping, hopping and skipping actions.	Select children to perform light bouncy jumps, high springy jumps, high skipping and long skipping – draw attention to feet together, light quick bounces, bent knees on take-off and landings, arms to lift and so on.
3	Select a jumping, hopping or skipping action, and, on the sound of the tambour, change your action.	Do this several times. Select some children to demonstrate, and highlight good body tension and coordination.
4	Decide when to change your action and this time, on the sound of the tambour, also add a change of direction or level.	Verbalise the children's choices so the ideas are shared.

Floor work

	Content	Teaching points
1	Sit with your legs out straight and rock from side to side.	The children should keep their hands in the air and hold strong body tension.
2	Find other parts of the body that you can rock on.	Select two or three children to demonstrate, and ask the class to try to copy their actions. The children should describe what they need to do in order to rock.
3	Rock on your bottom and then on your back.	The children should keep their arms tucked and gather momentum so they can stand up. Select some children to demonstrate.
4	Roll sideways (tucked) and then stretch out.	Discourage the children from covering their eyes – model this or select a child to demonstrate.
5	Choose whether you rock or roll. Can you do one action and then the other?	Select some children to show their sequences (several at a time, so that all the children have the opportunity to show). The other children should watch and describe rocking or rolling actions.

Apparatus

	Content	Teaching points
1	Use the floor space to explore jumping, hopping and skipping actions, linking them in sequences. When you come to the apparatus, find places where you can rock from one part of your body to another.	Circulate and verbalise the children's responses (for example, 'Jane is hopping and jumping, bending her knees and rocking on her bottom on the bench').
2	Use the floor space to explore jumping, hopping and skipping actions, linking them in sequences. When you come to the apparatus, find places where you can rock from one part of your body to another. Get off and find a way of rolling across the mat.	Select some children to demonstrate, and ask the others to watch and describe either the rocking or rolling action. Highlight good body tension.

Cool-down/calming down

Rock on your back, quicken your action and then gradually slow it down, until you come to a stop.

Classroom

Identify what the children thought they did well and what they need to do to improve for the next lesson.

SESSION 10
Assessment activity

This session is for interim assessment. It is intentionally very similar to the first assessment, in Session 1, so that the teacher can evaluate the children's progress. There is only floor work.

ASSESSMENT TASK

Select two ways of travelling and link these in a short sequence. Combine the actions with a starting and finishing body shape/action.

DISCUSSION

Ask the children to identify the changes that happen to the body during activity, and the benefits of being active to their health and well-being.

ASSESSMENT CRITERIA – QUESTIONS TO CONSIDER

1   Can the children perform two travelling actions and combine them in a sequence?

2   Can they add a starting and finishing shape/action, and remember and repeat their sequence with consistency, coordination and control (for example, arms and legs straight, toes and fingers stretched, body shapes held with good strong tension)?

3   Do they know what changes happen to their bodies when they are active, and the benefits of being active to their health and well-being?

4   Can they follow instructions and solve problems (for example, select travelling actions and add to a sequence)?

OUTCOME

Some children will achieve, some will excel and some will achieve less.

Warm-up

	Content	Teaching points
1	Play the 'Bean Game'. [Children move around the hall according to the bean that is called out: runner bean – running; jumping bean – jumping; chilli bean – rubbing all body parts to keep warm; jelly bean – wobbling like jelly; frozen bean – being still; baked bean – lying down as if looking at the sky; and butter bean – slide on your bottom.]	Verbalise the children's body actions, and highlight where they are demonstrating stretched and tensed bodies and good control.

Floor work

	Content	Teaching points
1	Explore a starting position that you can combine with a travelling action. Practise and refine this exercise.	Select some children to demonstrate, and highlight interesting body shapes, good body tension, stretched toes and fingers, and so on.
2	Hold your starting position and, on the sound of the tambour, add your travelling action. Can you add another action/ movement? Remember your sequence and add something that you have tried in a previous lesson (for example, slide, spin, rock or roll). Practise and refine this so you remember the sequence.	Select some children to demonstrate, and highlight interesting body shapes, good body tension, stretched toes and fingers, smooth transition of movements, and change in direction, levels and/or speed. Circulate and set differentiated challenges to accommodate individual abilities. For example, some children may be adding more movements/actions to their sequences, and combining with changes in direction levels and speed.
3	In pairs, names yourselves as 1 or 2. 1 should show his/her sequence to 2, and then change places. See if you can combine two actions in a sequence with a starting and finishing shape/action.	The children should provide feedback to each other about what they have included in their sequence. Encourage the children to share their achievements and ways forward at the end of the lesson.
	ASSESSMENT – By the teacher (in conjunction with a teaching assistant, where applicable), and also peer assessment by the children. Use ICT to record as many performances as possible so the children can self-assess during the lesson and in the classroom. This can also be kept as a record of their achievement.	

Cool-down/calming down
Walk around the room, stretch up high and curl up tightly. Wait until you are tapped and then line up. [*Enrol some children to help.*]

Classroom
Identify what the children thought they did well and what they need to do to improve for the next lesson.

SESSION 11
Big and small

Consolidation from previous session: to rock and roll on different body parts and combine in a sequence; to describe another's actions; to lift, carry and place equipment safely.

LEARNING OBJECTIVES

The objectives of the session need to be made explicit to the children. They also need to assess the extent to which they have achieved them.

Physical

1 To know that, by making themselves big, they take up more space.

2 To revise and learn a variety of stepping actions.

Well-being

3 To know about physical similarities and differences in others – and why this is important.

Broader learning

4 To move around without colliding, and to know why this is important.

ASSESSMENT CRITERIA – QUESTIONS TO CONSIDER

1 Are the children able to hold big and small body positions?

2 Can they combine big and small steps to make a movement pattern?

3 Do they know about physical similarities and differences in others (for example, height), and why this is important?

4 Are they able to move around without colliding, and know why this is important?

Warm-up

	Content	Teaching points
1	Run in and out of each other and change direction on the sound of the tambour.	Remind the children what we mean by 'in and out' and demonstrate good body control when changing direction.
2	Find another way of moving in and out of each other (skipping, hopping, jumping and so on). When you hear the tambour, either change direction or change level.	Verbalise the children's different actions and select some to show the class. Highlight bent knees, the use of arms, good body tension, watching where they are going and so on. Ask why this is important.

Floor work

	Content	Teaching points
1	Walk anywhere taking big steps.	Encourage the children to put their feet down heavily and then quietly.
2	Walk anywhere taking small steps.	Encourage the children to put their feet down heavily and then quietly.
3	Find a way of travelling while making yourself big.	Explain that, by being big, you take up a big space. Share the children's movement ideas.
4	Find a way of being still in a small position.	Select examples for the rest of the class to watch. Discuss with the children what they are seeing.
5	Walk around taking either big or small steps. Take four big steps and hold a big position. Then take four small steps and hold a small position.	The children should practise and refine their sequences. Circulate and give formative feedback so the children know what they have to do to improve (for example, good body tension). The children should share their performances with the class. They should identify, from examples, where children are holding clear positions that are either big or small.

Apparatus

	Content	Teaching points
1	Explore big and small steps, and make yourself big and small on the floor and apparatus (across, between, over, under, along and through).	Circulate and comment on what you see (for example, 'Tom is making a very big shape on the climbing frame by spreading his arms wide'). The children should show the rest of the class, and the class should identify where there are examples of good body tension.

Cool-down/calming down

Find a space and make yourself into a big shape slowly (to the count of eight). Change into a tucked small shape and make yourself as small as you can.

Classroom

Identify what the children thought they did well and what they need to do to improve for the next lesson.

SESSION 12
High and low

Consolidation from previous session: to explore big and small steps, lightly and heavily; to lift, carry and place equipment safely.

LEARNING OBJECTIVES

The objectives of the session need to be made explicit to the children. They also need to assess the extent to which they have achieved them.

Physical

1   To be able to perform actions at different levels.

2   To be able to combine 'like' actions in a sequence.

Well-being

3   To know about physical similarities and differences in others – and why this is important.

Broader learning

4   To be able to talk about how their movements have improved.

ASSESSMENT CRITERIA – QUESTIONS TO CONSIDER

1   Can the children perform actions at different levels?

2   Can they combine 'like' actions in a sequence?

3   Do they know about physical similarities and differences in others (for example, height), and why this is important?

4   Can they talk about how their movements have improved?

Warm-up

	Content	Teaching points
1	Run in and out of each other, and, on the sound of the tambour, take big steps (one strike) and take small steps (two strikes).	Ask the children how they will avoid a collision. Encourage the children to make steps fast and slow, and light and heavy.
2	Run in and out of each other, and, on the sound of the tambour, make yourself into a big shape (one strike) and make yourself into a small shape (two strikes).	Add commands of change of direction, change of speed and change of level. Select children who are making interesting big and small shapes to demonstrate to the rest of the class.
3	Run in and out of each other, taking big steps and small steps, and, on the sound of the tambour, hold a big or small shape for the count of three.	Verbalise the children's responses.

Floor work

	Content	Teaching points
1	Walk and lift your legs high as you go.	You or a child should demonstrate the 'in front and behind' motion.
2	Walk low near the floor.	The children should bend their knees. Choose a child to demonstrate. Ask the children what they have to do to keep their balance.
3	On the spot, spring high in the air.	The children should bend their knees on take-off and landing, and use their arms to lift up high.
4	Jump low near the floor.	The children should begin in a crouched position. Ask them what they have to do to keep their balance.
5	Add a starting position and now jump. Try again, but this time hold your starting position before you jump high and then low. Practise so you remember.	Circulate and set individual goals for children.
6	Find a partner. Name yourselves 1 and 2. 1 should show their sequence to 2, and then change places.	The children should say what they like about their partner's sequence.

Apparatus

	Content	Teaching points
1	Explore high and low positions on the floor and apparatus.	Circulate and comment on what you see (for example, 'Sarah is making herself very low while travelling along the bench by crouching down').

Cool-down/calming down
Stand in a space and stretch your fingers high. Slowly, to the count of ten, make yourself into a low shape, with all body parts tightly tucked.

Classroom
Identify what the children thought they did well and what they need to do to improve for the next lesson.

SESSION 13
Wide and narrow

Consolidation from previous session: to perform actions at different levels; to lift, carry and place equipment safely.

LEARNING OBJECTIVES

The objectives of the session need to be made explicit to the children. They also need to assess the extent to which they have achieved them.

Physical

1   To adapt movements on narrow and wide surfaces.

2   To remember and replicate a sequence.

Well-being

3   To know why being active is good for physical development.

Broader learning

4   To work as part of a team when getting out equipment.

ASSESSMENT CRITERIA – QUESTIONS TO CONSIDER

1   Can the children change their movements to fit on narrow and wide places?

2   Can they perform a short sequence that they have remembered?

3   Can they talk about why being active is good for physical development?

4   Do they work as part of a team when getting out equipment?

Warm-up

	Content	Teaching points
1	Move in and out of each other using all the space. When I strike the tambour once, jump up high. When I strike the tambour twice, jump down low.	Jump with the children and draw attention to feet together and change of level.
2	Jump in and out of each other using all the space. When I strike the tambour, change your direction.	Select some children to demonstrate changes in direction (forwards, sideways, backwards and diagonal).
3	Jump in and out of each other using all the space. When I strike the tambour, you choose whether to change either your level or your direction.	Verbalise the children's responses.

Floor work

	Content	Teaching points
1	Walk along a narrow line on the floor. [*Select markings or pretend there is a line.*]	The children should place one foot carefully in front of the other and keep their eyes focussed ahead, using their arms to balance.
2	Slide along a narrow line on the floor on your tummy, back and side. [*Select one way at a time.*]	Select some children to demonstrate and encourage the rest of the class to copy the ideas.
3	Travel on your hands and feet with them wide apart.	Select one or two examples for the rest of the class to watch and describe what they have seen.
4	Hold a starting shape and, on the count of three, travel on your hands and feet with them wide apart.	The children should practise this so that they remember it.
5	Hold a starting shape and, on the count of three, travel with your hands and feet wide apart, and then slide, making your body narrow.	The children should practise, refine and show a partner. Circulate and give the children individual formative feedback. Use a mini plenary (children's demonstrations) to share ideas and expectations.

Apparatus

	Content	Teaching points
1	Explore different ways of travelling on the floor by making your body wide and narrow, and, when you come to the apparatus, use some of these actions on wide and narrow parts of the apparatus.	Circulate and comment on what you see (for example, 'Peter is sliding on the wide bench on his back' or 'Salma is balancing along the narrow balance bar by placing one foot carefully in front of the other, and using her arms to help her balance').

Cool-down/calming down
Make yourself as wide as you can and then slowly make yourself into a tall narrow line. Hold your shape still.

Classroom
Identify what the children thought they did well and what they need to do to improve for the next lesson.

SESSION 14

Being aware of body parts – touching the floor with different body parts

Consolidation from previous session: to perform actions with wide and narrow body shapes; to lift, carry and place equipment safely.

LEARNING OBJECTIVES

The objectives of the session need to be made explicit to the children. They also need to assess the extent to which they have achieved them.

Physical

1   To identify light and heavy movements.

2   To remember a sequence of movements.

Well-being

3   To consciously name different body parts that are used during gymnastic activity.

Broader learning

4   To be able to solve movement problems independently.

ASSESSMENT CRITERIA – QUESTIONS TO CONSIDER

1   Can the children move around lightly and heavily on their feet?

2   Can they replicate a sequence?

3   Can they consciously name parts of the body they are using when moving?

4   Are the children able to solve movement problems by selecting actions and combine them in a sequence?

Warm-up

	Content	Teaching points
1	Travel in and out of each other on tiptoes.	Encourage the children to name which part of the foot they are using.
2	Travel in and out of each other on your heels.	Encourage the children to identify how their movement has changed. Select some children to demonstrate and encourage the rest of the class to say whether the movements are light or heavy.
3	Travel on any other part of your foot.	Select some children to demonstrate. Encourage the rest of the class to describe what they see.
4	Run in and out of each other, making light steps.	The children should describe how they travel and on which body part. Encourage them to move in and out of each other, and ask them what they have to do to ensure their steps are light.

	Content	Teaching points
5	Run in and out of each other, making your steps heavy.	Encourage the children to move in and out of each other, and ask them what they have to do to make their steps heavy.
6	Run in and out of each other, making your steps either light or heavy. On the sound of the tambour, change your stepping pattern (light to heavy or vice versa).	Select one or two responses to show the rest of the class.

Floor work

	Content	Teaching points
1	While standing, lean over and touch the floor lightly with your fingers, and then with your head.	Tell the children to keep their legs wide and knees bent. Ask them what might happen.
2	Touch the floor with one elbow and then the other elbow.	Ask they children if they can touch the floor with their wrists, knuckles, knees and ankles? Emphasise control.
3	Find other parts of your body to tap lightly on the floor.	Select a few examples for the class to watch. Discuss with the children what they have seen.
4	Make a phrase of tapping the floor with different parts of your body. Practise this so you remember it.	Tell the children to perform their action to the count of three and then to change their action. Select a few children to demonstrate. Highlight when they change from one action to another. Ask them if they can start with an interesting low-level body shape.
5	Get into pairs. Name yourselves 1 and 2. 1 should share his/her sequence with 2, and then change places.	Encourage the children who are watching to name the body parts that their partner is using to tap the floor.

Apparatus

	Content	Teaching points
1	Explore the floor area by running lightly and heavily on different parts of your foot. When you come to the apparatus, find places where you can have part of your body on the apparatus and touch the floor with another part.	Circulate and verbalise the children's responses (for example, 'Amid is travelling lightly on his toes on the floor, and pulling himself along the bench with his hands on the floor'). Encourage continuous movement.

Cool-down/calming down

Repeat the tapping phrase you made earlier as loud as you can and gradually get quieter until you can hardly hear a sound.

Classroom

Identify what the children thought they did well and what they need to do to improve for the next lesson.

Being aware of body parts – travelling on hands and feet

Consolidation from previous session: to name body parts, and select actions to refine, remember and perform in a sequence; to lift, carry and place equipment safely.

LEARNING OBJECTIVES

The objectives of the session need to be made explicit to the children. They also need to assess the extent to which they have achieved them.

Physical

1   To learn to balance on hands and feet.

2   To know and demonstrate a range of ways of travelling on hands and feet.

Well-being

3   To practise and work independently.

Broader learning

4   To share and learn from others' ideas.

ASSESSMENT CRITERIA – QUESTIONS TO CONSIDER

1   Are the children able to control their movements when balancing on their hands and feet?

2   Can they show two or three ways of moving on their hands and feet?

3   Are they able to work on a task independently?

4   Are they able to share and learn from others' ideas?

Warm-up

	Content	Teaching points
1	Travel in and out of each other lightly on your feet.	Encourage the children to change direction, speed and level.
2	Travel in and out of each other with heavy movements.	Encourage the children to change direction, speed and level.
3	Run in and out of each other, and, on the sound of the tambour, touch the floor with your elbows, hands, fingers, wrists and so on.	Highlight good body control as children move in and out, and reinforce how important it is to be aware of others to avoid collisions.
4	Run in and out of each other, and, on the sound of the tambour, touch the floor with a body part of your choice.	Do this several times and highlight the children's different ideas, encouraging the children to try them out.

Floor work

	Content	Teaching points
1	Find several ways of travelling along on your feet.	Encourage changes in direction (forwards, backwards, sideways and diagonal).
2	Find several ways of travelling along on your hands and feet.	Encourage changes in direction (forwards, backwards, sideways and diagonal). Select some children to demonstrate, and highlight that good body tension aids balance.
3	Find a way of travelling on your feet for the count of three, and then take your weight on your hands and feet for the count of three. Practise this on your own.	Select two or three children to demonstrate. Encourage the children to describe the two movements they are performing in their sequence.
4	Add a starting shape to your sequence. Now hold your starting position, and then travel on your feet for the count of three. Change, taking your weight on your hands and feet for the count of three. Repeat and practise this on your own.	Identify children who are changing from one shape to another to demonstrate, and draw attention to changes of actions.
5	A group of five or six children should perform their sequences. [*The rest of the class should watch. Repeat with another group (and another, if time allows).*]	The class should watch each group in turn. Encourage the children to identify movements they liked in each other's performances and to describe them.

Apparatus

	Content	Teaching points
1	Explore the floor space by taking your weight on your hands and feet. At the apparatus, explore using your hands and feet to travel along, over and around the apparatus.	Circulate and verbalise the children's responses.

Cool-down/calming down

Walk around on your hands and feet as quickly as you can, gradually getting slower, and then 'melt slowly into the ground'.

Classroom

Identify what the children thought they did well and what they need to do to improve for the next lesson.

SESSION 16

Travelling on different body parts

Consolidation from previous session: to take weight on hands and feet; to combine actions in a sequence; to lift, carry and place equipment safely.

LEARNING OBJECTIVES

The objectives of the session need to be made explicit to the children. They also need to assess the extent to which they have achieved them.

Physical

1   To continue to learn to travel on different body parts.

2   To know how to hold, still and clearly, a starting position.

Well-being

3   To know about the changes that happen to the body when active.

Broader learning

4   To listen to and show consideration for others when watching their work.

ASSESSMENT CRITERIA – QUESTIONS TO CONSIDER

1   Can the children travel on two or three body parts?

2   Are they able to incorporate a clear and still starting position into their sequence?

3   Can they talk about the changes that happen to the body when active?

4   Do they listen to and show consideration for others when watching their work?

Warm-up

	Content	Teaching points
1	Move around the room, taking your weight on your feet and hands.	Verbalise responses (for example, 'Lauren is taking the weight on her hands and feet, and her tummy is facing the ceiling' and 'Michael has his tummy facing the floor').
2	Watch the two children picked to demonstrate. Try one of their ways of travelling.	Select two children to demonstrate their movement, and highlight good body tension.
3	Continue travelling and, when I clap my hands, change so that your tummy is facing the other way.	Verbalise responses.
4	Move around the hall and, on the sound of the tambour, change the direction of your movement.	Circulate and verbalise forwards, backwards, sideways and diagonal movements (for example, 'Laila is moving with her hands and feet moving forwards and her tummy facing the ceiling').

Floor work

	Content	Teaching points
1	Choose a way of moving around the floor on any part of your body.	Select some children to demonstrate a range of ideas, which the rest of the class should then try. Encourage the children to watch carefully and select one idea that they want to try.
2	Select a way of travelling that you like. Perform it with a change of direction.	Select one or two children to demonstrate, and verbalise directional changes.
3	Select a starting body shape you can hold still and, when I say 'go', add the travelling movement you have been practising. Now change the direction of your movement. Practise so that you know your sequence.	Circulate and verbalise responses, giving individual formative feedback.
4	With a partner, name yourselves 1 and 2. 2 should show his/her sequence to 1. Hold your starting position and go. Now change over, and 1 should show his/her sequence to 2. Is your partner able to hold his/her starting shape still?	Encourage the children to identify what their partner is doing well. Reinforce tension in the body.

Apparatus

	Content	Teaching points
1	Travel on the floor and on the apparatus with different parts of the body.	Verbalise responses (for example, 'Jim is sliding along the bench on his tummy' and 'Adam is taking his weight on his hands and feet on the floor'). Encourage the children to keep their movement continuous.

Cool-down/calming down
Stretch up high, and then curl down your body on to your knees. Lie down on your tummy and roll over, keeping very still. Wait until you are touched on your foot to line up.

Classroom
Identify what the children thought they did well and what they need to do to improve for the next lesson.

Keeping still while on hands and feet

Consolidation from previous session: to travel on different body parts; to add a starting position that can be held still at the beginning of a sequence; to lift, carry and place equipment safely.

LEARNING OBJECTIVES

The objectives of the session need to be made explicit to the children. They also need to assess the extent to which they have achieved them.

Physical

1   To know when the body is tense and when it is relaxed.

2   To continue to learn to balance on hands and feet.

Well-being

3   To continue to develop an understanding of the changes that happen to the body during activity, and the benefits of this to physical health.

Broader learning

4   To work as a team to lift, carry and place equipment.

ASSESSMENT CRITERIA – QUESTIONS TO CONSIDER

1   Are the children aware of when their bodies are tense and when they are relaxed?

2   Do they use body tension to help them balance?

3   Are they able to talk about some of the changes that happen to the body during activity, and the benefits of this to physical health?

4   Are they able to work as a team to lift, carry and place equipment?

Warm-up

	Content	Teaching points
1	Travel in and out of each other on your feet.	Encourage running, jumping, hopping and skipping. Verbalise the children's responses and encourage them to change their movement on the sound of the tambour.
2	Travel in and out of each other on your hands and feet.	Verbalise the children's responses and encourage them to change their movement on the sound of the tambour.
3	Find another body part to travel on (tummy, back, knees, sides and so on).	Verbalise the children's responses and encourage them to change their movement on the sound of the tambour.

Floor work

	Content	Teaching points
1	Put your hands and feet on the floor and keep absolutely still.	The children's hands should be flat on the floor, they should stretch their body and try to get tension throughout the body.
2	Put two hands and one foot on the floor and keep absolutely still.	The children's hands should be flat on the floor, they should stretch their body and try to get tension throughout the body.
3	Put one hand and two feet on the floor, keeping very still.	The children's hands should be flat on the floor, they should stretch their body and try to get tension throughout the body.
4	Put one hand and one foot on the floor, keeping very still.	The children's hands should be flat on the floor, they should stretch their body and try to get tension throughout the body.
5	Select one of these balances and, on the count of three, change to another of them.	A group of five or six children should demonstrate (individually) their actions to the rest of the class. Repeat with different children as appropriate. Encourage the children to watch and look for good body tension in others' movements. Ask them how they know when there is good body tension.

Apparatus

	Content	Teaching points
1	Explore, on the floor, ways of travelling on different body parts, then, when you come to the apparatus, find places where you can hold still shapes.	Circulate and comment on what your see (for example, 'Alesha is skipping sideways on the floor and balancing on the apparatus on one foot').

Cool-down/calming down

Balance on two hands and two feet, and then two hands and one foot (keep the other leg straight and toes stretched outwards). See if you can now balance on one foot and one hand. Hold for the count of five and then slowly move into a seated position (straight backs).

Classroom

Identify what the children thought they did well and what they need to do to improve for the next lesson.

SESSION 18

Holding stretched and tucked positions

Consolidation from previous session: to take weight on hands and feet; to combine actions to form a sequence; to lift, carry and place equipment safely.

LEARNING OBJECTIVES

The objectives of the session need to be made explicit to the children. They also need to assess the extent to which they have achieved them.

Physical

1   To know how to stretch and tuck the body, and hold good body tension.

2   To combine tucking and stretching actions in a sequence.

Well-being

3   To know and understand the importance of changing into the correct clothing for PE (with long hair tied back).

Broader learning

4   To work as a team to lift, carry and place equipment.

ASSESSMENT CRITERIA – QUESTIONS TO CONSIDER

1   Can the children perform stretching and tucking actions, and know the difference between the two?

2   Can they combine these actions in a sequence?

3   Can they talk about the importance of changing into the correct clothing for PE (with long hair tied back)?

4   Do they work as a team to lift, carry and place equipment?

Warm-up

	Content	Teaching points
1	Move around the room, taking your weight on your hands and feet.	Encourage the children to show variety in their travelling actions.
2	Continue the movement and, on the sound of the tambour, find a different way of taking your weight on your hands and feet.	Verbalise the children's responses (for example, 'Susie is moving with her tummy facing the ceiling and then changing so her tummy is facing the floor').
3	Continue to do this and, on two strikes of the tambour, change direction.	Verbalise the children's responses as above.

Floor work

	Content	Teaching points
1	While on your hands and feet, stretch your body as far as possible.	Encourage the children to stretch all parts of the body, and draw attention to fingers and toes.
2	While on your hands and feet, tuck your body up as tight as possible.	Select some children to demonstrate good stretched positions and good tucked positions. Discuss the difference with the children.
3	Choose part of your body to be still on, and then stretch all the other parts out as far as possible. Then tuck up.	Emphasise body tension and control.
4	Now stretch, tuck and stretch. Practise and refine your sequence.	Encourage the children to work with a partner, and to say what is good about their partner's stretch and tuck.

Apparatus

	Content	Teaching points
1	Move on the floor, taking your weight on your hands and feet. When you come to the apparatus, find places where you can stretch and tuck.	Circulate and comment on what you see. Give formative feedback to individual children to help them improve.

Cool-down/calming down
Stretch up high and slowly, to the count of eight, and then change into a tucked position.

Classroom
Identify what the children thought they did well and what they need to do to improve for the next lesson.

Moving in extended and tucked positions

Consolidation from previous session: to know how to stretch and tuck the body; to combine actions to make a sequence; to lift, carry and place equipment safely.

LEARNING OBJECTIVES

The objectives of the session need to be made explicit to the children. They also need to assess the extent to which they have achieved them.

Physical

1   To know when the body is stretched (extended) and when it is tucked.

2   To be able to give feedback to peers against set criteria.

Well-being

3   To reinforce the importance of changing into the correct clothing for PE.

Broader learning

4   To follow instructions in answer to movement problems.

ASSESSMENT CRITERIA – QUESTIONS TO CONSIDER

1   Can the children perform actions where they stretch or tuck?

2   Can they identify stretching or tucking actions in their peers' performances and say what is good about them?

3   Can they explain the importance of changing into the correct clothing for PE?

4   Can they follow instructions in answer to movement problems set by the teacher?

Warm-up

	Content	Teaching points
1	Run in and out of each other, and, on the sound of the tambour, tuck up small.	Highlight the criteria of good performance (for example, 'Rosie has tucked her arms and knees tightly into her body').
2	Jump in and out of each other, and, on the sound of the tambour, stretch out wide.	As above, highlight the criteria of good performance (for example, 'Eben has straight arms and fingers as he stretches up high').
3	Skip in and out of each other, and, on the sound of the tambour, decide whether to stretch or tuck.	Emphasise clear, held positions.

Floor work

	Content	Teaching points
1	Spring into the air. Stretch your body while in the air.	Emphasise control and tension throughout the body.
2	Travel on your hands and feet, stretching your arms and legs as you go along.	Show the work of children who are performing good stretches. Draw attention to why their work is good.
3	Travel on your hands and feet, keeping your body tucked up.	Show the work of children who are performing good tucked positions. Draw attention to why their work is good.
4	Travel on your hands and feet, stretching your arms and legs as you go. Then change into a tucked position while you are travelling along.	Select children to demonstrate and ask the children what they like about the ideas.
5	Get into pairs and show each other your sequence. Tell your partner when their arms and legs are really straight.	Circulate and comment on what you see. Give formative feedback to individual children to help them to improve.

Apparatus

	Content	Teaching points
1	Travel on the floor on your hands and feet, and explore the apparatus to see where you can move into stretched and tucked positions.	Circulate and comment on what you see (for example, 'Paul is jumping off the horse, stretching up high and landing with bent knees').

Cool-down/calming down

In a space, tuck up tightly, and then stretch out as I count up to ten. Stand up tall and then tuck up tightly again.

Classroom

Identify what the children thought they did well and what they need to do to improve for the next lesson.

SESSION 20
Final assessment activity

This session will assess children's knowledge and understanding gained from the sessions throughout the year. Children should be encouraged to take responsibility for their own learning by identifying what they can achieve, what they need to do to develop and how they will do this.

ASSESSMENT TASKS

On the floor

Select two 'like' ways of travelling on different body parts with contrasting body shapes (for example, jumping high and then low, wide and narrow, big and small, stretched and tucked). Link these in a short sequence and practise the sequence so it can be remembered and performed well.

Add a starting body shape and finishing shape, or action, to the sequence.

On the apparatus

Explore the apparatus, transferring the same actions from the floor on to the apparatus.

DISCUSSION

Talk about what changes happen to the body when it is active, and the benefits of being active to your health and well-being.

Describe the new skills you have learned.

Discuss your work and say what you might do to make it even better.

ASSESSMENT CRITERIA – QUESTIONS TO CONSIDER

1 Can the children perform two travelling actions and combine them with contrasting body shapes in a sequence?

2 Can they add a starting shape and a finishing shape, or action?

3 Can they remember and perform the sequence with consistency, coordination and control?

4 Can they talk about the changes that happen to their bodies when they are active, and the benefits of being active to their health and well-being?

5 Can they talk about the new skills they have learned?

6 Can they identify actions/movements that they can perform well and know one or two ways in which they can improve?

OUTCOME

Some children will achieve, some will excel and some will achieve less.

Warm-up

	Content	Teaching points
1	Play the 'Bean Game'. [*See Session 10 from Year 1, page 96.*]	Verbalise the children's body actions, and highlight where they are demonstrating good control and tension.

Floor work

	Content	Teaching points
1	Remember all the different ways that you have travelled around the hall. On the sound of the tambour, select one and, when you hear the tambour again, change it so you perform it in a different way.	Encourage the children to perform several different travelling actions and verbalise these. Draw attention to the variety of ways that actions/movements can be performed (for example, wide and narrow, high and low, big and small, pushing and pulling, and stretched and tucked).
2	Add a starting position and combine it with your two travelling actions. Practise and refine.	Show and highlight interesting body shapes, good body tension, stretched toes and fingers, and so on. Ask the children what they can do well and what they need to do to improve.
3	Hold your starting position and, on the sound of the tambour, show me your sequence. Add an interesting finishing action to complete your sequence. Practise and refine so you remember the sequence.	Select some children to demonstrate, and highlight interesting body shapes, good body tension, stretched toes and fingers, smooth transition of movements, and changes in direction, level and/or speed.
4	In pairs, name yourselves 1 and 2. 2 should show 1 his/her sequence, and then change places.	The children should describe each other's sequences and identify whether they have included a starting and finishing position.

Apparatus

	Content	Teaching points
1	Find a space on the floor and travel using the same movements that you have been combining in your sequence. When you get to the apparatus, explore whether you can perform these actions/movements on to, along, over and off the apparatus.	Verbalise the responses.
	ASSESSMENT – By the teacher (in conjunction with a teaching assistant where applicable), and also peer assessment by the children. Use ICT to record as many performances as possible so the children can self-assess during the lesson and in the classroom. This can also be kept as a record of their achievement.	

Cool-down/calming down

Walk around the room, stretch up high and curl up tightly. Wait until you are tapped and then line up. [*Enrol some children to help.*]

Classroom

Identify what the children thought they did well and what they need to do to improve for the next lesson.

'Explore pushing and pulling actions on the floor, and find ways where you can slide on the apparatus.'

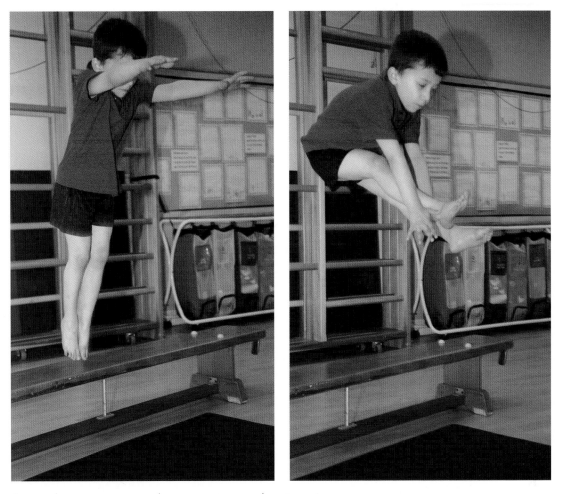

'. . . when you come to the apparatus, explore jumping on
to, along, over and off.'

The sessions
Year 2

SESSION 1
Assessment activity

This session is intentionally similar to Session 20 from Year 1 so that the teacher can re-assess and reflect on the impact the summer break and transition into Year 2 has had on the children's progress. It is possible that growth spurts may also have impacted on their skill level. There is both floor and apparatus work.

ASSESSMENT TASKS

On the floor

Select two 'like' ways of travelling on different body parts with contrasting body shapes (for example, jumping high and then low, wide and narrow, big and small, stretched and tucked). Link these in a short sequence and practise the sequence so it can be remembered and performed well. Add a starting body shape and finishing shape, or action, to the sequence.

On the apparatus

Explore the apparatus, transferring the same actions from the floor on to the apparatus.

DISCUSSION

Talk about what changes happen to the body when it is active, and the benefits of being active to your health and well-being.

Describe the new skills you have learned.

Discuss your work and say what you might do to make it even better.

ASSESSMENT CRITERIA – QUESTIONS TO CONSIDER

1   Can the children perform two travelling actions and combine them with contrasting body shapes in a sequence?
2   Can they add a starting shape and a finishing shape, or action?
3   Can they remember and perform the sequence with consistency, coordination and control?
4   Can they talk about the changes that happen to their bodies when they are active, and the benefits of being active to their health and well-being?
5   Can they talk about the new skills they have learned?
6   Can they identify actions/movements that they can perform well and know one or two ways in which they can improve?

OUTCOME

Some children will achieve, some will excel and some will achieve less.

Warm-up

	Content	Teaching points
1	Play the 'Bean Game'. [See Session 10 from Year 1, page 96.]	Verbalise the children's body actions and highlight where they are demonstrating good control and tension.

Floor work

	Content	Teaching points
1	Remember all the different ways that you have travelled around the hall. On the sound of the tambour, select one and, when you hear the tambour again, change it so you perform it in a different way.	Encourage the children to perform several different travelling actions and verbalise these. Draw attention to the variety of ways that actions/movements can be performed (for example, wide and narrow, high and low, big and small, pushing and pulling, and stretched and tucked).
2	Add a starting position and combine with your two travelling actions. Practise and refine.	Show and highlight interesting body shapes, good body tension, stretched toes and fingers, and so on. Ask the children what they can do well and what they need to do to improve.
3	Hold your starting position and, on the sound of the tambour, show me your sequence. Add an interesting finishing action to complete your sequence. Practise and refine so you remember the sequence.	Circulate and set differentiated challenges to accommodate individual abilities. For example, some children may be adding more movements/actions to their sequence and combining with a change of direction, level or speed. Select some children to demonstrate, and highlight interesting body shapes, good body tension, stretched toes and fingers, smooth transition of movements, and changes in direction, level and/or speed.
4	In pairs, name yourselves 1 and 2. 2 should show 1 their sequence, and then change places.	The children should describe each other's sequences, and identify whether they have included a starting and finishing position.

Apparatus

	Content	Teaching points
1	Find a space on the floor and travel using the same movements that you have been combining in your sequence. When you get to the apparatus, explore whether you can perform these actions/movements on to, along, over and off the apparatus.	Verbalise the responses.
	ASSESSMENT – By the teacher (in conjunction with a teaching assistant where applicable), and also peer assessment by the children. Use ICT to record as many performances as possible so the children can self-assess during the lesson and in the classroom. This can also be kept as a record of their achievement.	

Cool-down/calming down
Walk around the room, stretch up high and curl up tightly. Wait until you are tapped and then line up. [*Enrol some children to help.*]

Classroom
Identify what the children thought they did well and what they need to do to improve for the next lesson.

SESSION 2

Handling apparatus safely

This session is to reinforce Session 2 from Year 1 'Handling apparatus safely' session so that the children are clear about the expectations for Year 2 (which should be progressive in terms of the children taking more responsibility).

LEARNING OBJECTIVES

The objectives of the session need to be made explicit to the children. They also need to assess the extent to which they have achieved them.

Physical

1   To know how to lift, carry and place apparatus safely.

2   To know that it is important to work as a team when lifting heavy equipment.

Well-being

3   To know why lifting, carrying and placing equipment safely is important to health and well-being.

Broader learning

4   To recognise and respond to issues of safety relating to themselves and others, and know how to get help.

ASSESSMENT CRITERIA – QUESTIONS TO CONSIDER

1   Are the children able to follow the teacher and leader's instructions when they lift, carry and place equipment?

2   Can they work as a team when they are lifting, carrying and placing equipment?

3   Can they discuss why they have to be careful when lifting, carrying and placing equipment?

4   Do they know that they should not get on any equipment until it is checked by the teacher, and that they should ask the teacher for help if and when required?

Warm-up

	Content	Teaching points
1	Run, jump, hop and skip in and out of each other. On the sound of the tambour, change from one movement into another.	Verbalise the different responses. Discuss with the children why it is important to warm-up before lifting, carrying and placing equipment.
2	Run in and out of each other and get into groups of three, then six, then eight and then four.	The children should organise themselves in the correct number. When in groups of four, the children should sit down in their group.

Apparatus organisation

	Content	Teaching points
1	Sit with legs crossed and with straight backs. Whoever is doing this well will be the leader.	Select some children to demonstrate straight backs and ask children if they remember when it is important to keep their backs straight (relate this to when lifting). Select the leaders.
2	How do we lift a bench safely?	One group should demonstrate. The leader of the group should take charge and all the other children should get out the benches. Two children should stand along each side of the bench, opposite one another. When the leader say 'lift', all the children should lift together, with legs slightly bent and backs straight. When the leader says 'move', the children should walk forwards towards where their group was sitting and, when leader says 'down', they should place the bench on the floor.
3	All groups should collect two mats.	The teacher should highlight where groups are working as a team. All lifting, moving and placing should be by instruction from the leader. When done, the children should balance on a part of their body of their choice (to accommodate different completion times).
4	All the groups should collect two other pieces of equipment (depending on what is available at the school, for example, a bar box, a trestle table, an agility plank or slide ladders). Place the pieces together to make the arrangement more interesting.	The groups should demonstrate lifting, carrying and placing of different equipment to the rest of the class. Highlight straight backs, slightly bent knees, all lifting, moving and placing being done by instruction of the leader, and working as a team member. Encourage the children to place the apparatus at different angles.
5	One group will get out the wall frame.	Select a group to get out the wall frame and demonstrate this task to the rest of the class. Highlight the importance of securing bolts, ladders and so on.
6	Depending on the individual equipment available, you will also need to show how to attach the various apparatus using Velcro®, hooks and bolts, and inform the children that the equipment *must* be checked by the teacher before they climb on to *any* of it. Try to angle the equipment to make it more interesting.	

Apparatus

	Content	Teaching points
I	Use the floor space to combine two or more travelling movements together and, when you come to the apparatus, explore these travelling movements (on to, along, over, across and off).	Verbalise the different responses and select some children to demonstrate. Do they need to adapt their movements? Can they do this? Encourage the children to return to their group and, on instruction from their leader, to return the equipment back to the original places.

Cool-down/calming down

Find a space and make yourself as small as you can. On the count of six, gradually unfold your body and stretch as high or as wide as possible. Hold yourself fully stretched and then slowly return to your original position.

Classroom

Identify what the children thought they did well and what they need to do to improve for the next lesson.

'Find a way of being still in a small position.'

'Now hold a balance using two hands and one foot.'

'Travel up to the apparatus in an interesting way and find places where you can hold interesting balances.'

Slide, spin, push, pull

Consolidation from previous session: to lift, carry and place equipment safely.

LEARNING OBJECTIVES

The objectives of the session need to be made explicit to the children. They also need to assess the extent to which they have achieved them.

Physical

1   To know how to perform sliding and spinning actions using the body to push and pull.

2   To recognise the differences when some actions are performed at different levels.

Well-being

3   To identify physical changes to the body during activity.

Broader learning

4   To be able to listen to and respond to their peers in a positive manner.

ASSESSMENT CRITERIA – QUESTIONS TO CONSIDER

1   Can the children perform a sliding and spinning action by pushing and/or pulling?

2   Can they recognise the differences when they perform actions at different levels?

3   Can they talk easily about physical changes that take place to their bodies when they are active?

4   Are they able to listen to and show consideration for others' views and, in some cases, feelings?

Warm-up

	Content	Teaching points
1	Run in and out of each other, and jump up high from time to time.	Highlight two feet together and bent knees on take-off and landing.
2	Do light bouncy jumps and, on the sound of the tambour, change to high springy jumps.	Select some children to perform the two different jumps. Encourage the children to highlight the differences.
3	Use a running action to dodge and swerve.	Discuss with the children how to do this (take small steps, turn the shoulders, lean and so on). Discuss where this skill is used in other PE areas (for example, games).
4	Run in and out of each other, and, on the sound of the tambour, swerve and change your direction of travel.	Select some children to demonstrate good practice.

Floor work

	Content	Teaching points
1	Use a sliding action to travel along the floor.	Encourage the children to slide on different parts of the body (for example, backs, tummies and bottoms).
2	Use a spinning action to turn round and round.	Highlight different levels that spins can be performed at (for example, on one foot, bottoms, knees and so on).
3	Use a pushing action to jump high in the air.	Encourage the children to push with their feet and knees on take-off and landing.
4	Use a pulling action to slide on your tummy.	Emphasise hands on the floor.
5	Select two actions from sliding, spinning, pushing or pulling, and link them together. Practise so you can remember the sequence.	Circulate and give the children individual feedback to encourage them to refine their actions.
6	In pairs, name yourselves 1 and 2. 1 should show 2 their sequence, and then change places.	Encourage the children to say what they like about their own and their partner's sequence. Ask them to talk about the levels their partner is using.

Apparatus

	Content	Teaching points
1	Find a space and hold an interesting shape on a magic spot. On the sound of the tambour, travel around the hall by either sliding, spinning, pushing or pulling, and, when you come to the apparatus, explore where you can slide, spin, push or pull. On two strikes of the tambour, travel back to the magic spot in a different way.	Circulate and highlight the children who are sliding, spinning pushing and pulling in different ways. Select one or two examples to watch and discuss with the class how the actions are being used.

Cool-down/calming down
Sit in a space, and spin round and round. Curl up and hold yourself still.

Classroom
Identify what the children thought they did well and what they need to do to improve for the next lesson.

SESSION 4
Jumping, hopping and skipping

Consolidation from previous session: to slide, spin, push and pull, and link two or more actions together; to lift, carry and place equipment safely.

LEARNING OBJECTIVES

The objectives of the session need to be made explicit to the children. They also need to assess the extent to which they have achieved them.

Physical

1   To be able to replicate actions in a sequence.

2   To develop an awareness of ways to make sequences more interesting to an audience.

Well-being

3   To identify the new skills they have learned.

Broader learning

4   To know some of the strengths in their work and be able to identify ways that will help them improve.

ASSESSMENT CRITERIA – QUESTIONS TO CONSIDER

1   Can the children replicate a sequence and use devices (change of level, speed and direction) to make their sequences more interesting to an audience?

2   Are they able to talk about the new skills they have learned?

3   Are they able to discuss some of their strengths and identify ways that will help them improve?

Warm-up

	Content	Teaching points
1	Slide on different parts of your body around the room. On the sound of the tambour, change from a pulling to a pushing action, or vice versa.	Verbalise the children's responses. Discuss with the children that, when they change direction, they are pushing or pulling.
2	Slide around the room and, on the sound of the tambour, add a spin.	Ask the children what they have to do to increase the speed of their spin.
3	Slide around the room and, on one strike of the tambour, change from a pulling to a pushing action, or vice versa, and, on two strikes of the tambour, add a spin.	Select some children to demonstrate, and highlight knees together while spinning.

Floor work

	Content	Teaching points
1	Use light bouncy jumps and high springy jumps to travel all over the floor, in and out of each other.	Emphasise slightly bent knees on take-off and landing. Verbalise the children's responses.
2	Use skipping to go around the room. On one strike of the tambour, jump, and, on two strikes, skip.	Encourage the children to identify criteria for developing their actions. For example, bent knees on take-off and landing, and good use of arms to aid lift.
3	Try hopping on one leg and then the other. Can you do a long hop? And now a high hop?	Emphasise the use of arms to aid lift.
4	Make up a sequence that includes a jump, a skip and a hop.	Encourage the children to change direction and re-order their sequence to make the performance more interesting.
5	In pairs, name yourselves 1 and 2. 2 should show 1 their sequence, and then change places.	The children should identify in each other's sequence where they are adding a change of direction. Encourage them to say what actions are used.

Apparatus

	Content	Teaching points
1	Start on a magic spot and travel towards the apparatus by jumping, skipping or hopping. When at the apparatus, explore where you can perform these actions on, along, over, across and off the apparatus.	Ask the children to decide which action they will use before they begin.
2	On the sound of the tambour, find a different way to return to your magic spot.	Select some children to demonstrate either individual actions on the apparatus or their combined sequences. Encourage the children to verbalise the actions.

Cool-down/calming down

Jump around the room and, on the sound of the tambour, slow down until you stop, and slowly curl down your body until you are tucked up tightly on the floor.

Classroom

Identify what the children thought they did well and what they need to do to improve for the next lesson.

SESSION 5
Using actions with rotation (turning)

Consolidation from previous session: to combine jumping, hopping and skipping actions in a sequence; to adapt movements on to the apparatus; to lift, carry and place equipment safely.

LEARNING OBJECTIVES

The objectives of the session need to be made explicit to the children. They also need to assess the extent to which they have achieved them.

Physical

1 To be able to replicate a sequence of actions.

2 To understand the terms 'rotate' and 'spin'.

Well-being

3 To know that healthy eating and physical activity are beneficial to health and well-being.

Broader learning

4 To know how attitude and behaviour may impact on others.

ASSESSMENT CRITERIA – QUESTIONS TO CONSIDER

1 Are the children able to remember and repeat actions in a sequence?

2 Can they perform a spin and rotating action?

3 Are they able to talk about how healthy eating and physical activity are beneficial to health and well-being?

4 Do they understand how their behaviour can impact on the relationships they have with others?

Warm-up

	Content	Teaching points
1	Jump around the room in and out of each other, and, on the sound of the tambour, change to a hop.	Emphasise bent knees on take-off and landing. Encourage the children to vary their jumping and hopping actions (for example, high, low, long and so on). Verbalise their responses.
2	Hop around the room and, on the sound of the tambour, change to a skip.	Encourage variations in actions (for example, long hops, and high and low skips).
3	Jump, hop or skip in and out of each other, and, on one strike of the tambour, change direction. On two strikes of the tambour, change level. On three strikes of the tambour, change action.	Select some children to demonstrate, and highlight changes in direction, level and action.

Floor work

	Content	Teaching points
1	Run in and out of each other, and, on the sound of the tambour, rotate all the way around.	Explain that 'rotate' means turn. Verbalise responses. Ask the children which part of their foot they balanced on to do this.
2	Run and, on the sound of the tambour, spin around while standing upright.	Ask the children which part of their foot they balanced on. Select one or two children who are spinning well to demonstrate. Encourage the children to balance on the ball of their foot and use their arms.
3	Sit and spin round and round.	Discuss with the children what they do to get faster.
4	Hold an interesting starting shape and, on the count of four ('ready, one, two, three, four'), rotate.	Use your voice to guide the children.
5	Hold an interesting starting shape and, on the count of four, spin ('ready, one, two, three, four, spin high, one, two, three, four, spin low'). Now practise your sequence.	Select one or two children to demonstrate. Encourage the children to add an interesting starting position.
6	With a partner, name yourselves either 1 or 2. 2 should hold their starting shape and, on 'go', show their sequence to 1. Then change places.	Encourage children to identify what they need to practise to improve, and what they like about each other's sequences.

Apparatus

	Content	Teaching points
1	Find a magic spot and hold your starting position. On 'go', run, change direction and spin (high and low). When you come to the apparatus, find places where you can turn round, spin or turn over on the apparatus.	Verbalise the children's responses.

Cool-down/calming down
Sit and spin round and round. Spin in the other direction. Then hold yourself still and tightly huddled until you are tapped on the shoulder. Then line up.

Classroom
Identify what the children thought they did well and what they need to do to improve for the next lesson.

SESSION 6

Travelling quickly or slowly

Consolidation from previous session: to rotate the body by spinning and turning at different levels; to lift, carry and place equipment safely.

LEARNING OBJECTIVES

The objectives of the session need to be made explicit to the children. They also need to assess the extent to which they have achieved them.

Physical

1   To be able to demonstrate the term 'gradual' as the speed quickens and slows in sequences.

2   To be able to discuss the criteria for holding good body control.

Well-being

3   To know why it is important to change clothing to be ready for physical activity.

Broader learning

4   To know the importance of moving safely around the hall and on apparatus.

ASSESSMENT CRITERIA – QUESTIONS TO CONSIDER

1   Can the children gradually quicken and slow their speed when asked to do so?

2   Are they able to identify some of the criteria for holding good body control?

3   Can they discuss why it is important to change their clothing to be ready for physical activity?

4   Are they consciously aware of others when working on the floor and apparatus?

Warm-up

	Content	Teaching points
1	Run and, on the sound of the tambour, spin low or rotate up high.	Verbalise the children's responses.
2	Run in and out of each other, and, on the sound of the tambour, spin and then change the direction or level of your spin.	Select one or two children to demonstrate, and highlight changes in level and direction.
3	Jump, hop or skip and, on the sound of the tambour, spin high or low.	As above, select one or two children to demonstrate, and highlight changes in level and direction.

Floor work

	Content	Teaching points
1	Run in and out of each other slowly, and, every time I strike the tambour, get a bit quicker.	Strike the tambour until the children are moving really fast. Then, ask them to slow down on each strike of the tambour. Verbalise the children's movements, drawing attention to the change in speed. Select two or three children to demonstrate.
2	Jump in and out of each other slowly, and, every time I strike the tambour, get a bit quicker.	Strike the tambour until children are moving really fast. Then, ask them to slow down on each strike of the tambour. Encourage them not to lose the quality of their jumps. Emphasise feet together and bending knees on take-off and landing.
3	Travel slowly on your hands and feet, and, on the sound of the tambour, quicken the pace, and then gradually slow down as before.	Encourage the children to keep to the pace of the tambour beat.
4	Hold an interesting starting position and, on the instruction 'go', run, jump and run again, changing the speed of these actions until you come to a stop.	Select some children with good body control to demonstrate. Ask the children why body control is important.
5	Now we will show each other our sequences. [*Half the children should show their sequence to the rest of the class, and then change places.*]	Encourage each child to focus on a specific individual and identify the change of speed in that child's movements.

Apparatus

	Content	Teaching points
1	Find a magic spot and hold an interesting starting position. On 'go', run or jump up to the apparatus, and move on, along and over it, either quickly or slowly (but safely). On the sound of the tambour, jump off the apparatus and run quickly back to your magic spot.	Select one or two examples for the rest of the class to watch. Discuss with the children what they saw and why it was good work.

Cool-down/calming down
Tuck up small in a space and then gradually stretch out as far as possible. Tuck up small in a space again and then stretch out quickly. Finish by standing tall.

Classroom
Identify what the children thought they did well and what they need to do to improve for the next lesson.

Strongly and lightly

Consolidation from previous session: to perform movements with varied speeds; to lift, carry and place equipment safely.

LEARNING OBJECTIVES

The objectives of the session need to be made explicit to the children. They also need to assess the extent to which they have achieved them.

Physical

1   To know that movements and actions can be performed strongly and lightly.

2   To be able to share movement ideas with a partner.

Well-being

3   To identify how the body feels during and after activity.

Broader learning

4   To know what has to be done to improve performance.

ASSESSMENT CRITERIA – QUESTIONS TO CONSIDER

1   Can the children differentiate their movements so that they can perform them both lightly and strongly?

2   Are they able to share movement ideas with a partner?

3   Can they talk about how their bodies feel during and after activity?

4   Are they able to identify one or two criteria for developing their performances?

Warm-up

	Content	Teaching points
1	Run in and out of each other, and, on one strike of the tambour, slow down. On two strikes of the tambour, get quicker.	Emphasise the difference between quicker and slower. Verbalise the children's responses.
2	Jump in and out of each other, and, on the sound of the tambour, slow down. On two strikes of the tambour, get quicker.	As above, emphasise the difference between quicker and slower. Verbalise the children's responses.
3	Skip in and out of each other, and, on one strike of the tambour, slow down. On two strikes of the tambour, get quicker.	As above, emphasise the difference between quicker and slower. Verbalise the children's responses.
4	Choose how to move, and, on one strike of the tambour, slow down. On two strikes of the tambour, get quicker.	Verbalise the children's responses.

Floor work

	Content	Teaching points
1	Use a lot of strength to spring high in the air.	Emphasise the use of arms to help, and bending knees slightly on take-off and landing.
2	Use your feet in a variety of ways to travel lightly all over the floor.	Look at a few examples with the children. Discuss ways of using feet.
3	Lie on your tummy, pushing strongly with your hands to perform a sliding action.	Select one or two children to demonstrate. Encourage the children to note the use of the arms.
4	Find other ways of pushing or pulling strongly with your hands to do a sliding action.	Emphasise holding the body in a strong position.
5	With a partner, find a low starting position that you can both hold, and then go into a slide, using your hands to push or pull.	Discuss whether the children are travelling towards, away in opposite directions, or in the same direction.
6	Practise and refine. Finish by springing up high.	Circulate and give individual formative feedback.
7	Partners should show their sequences. [Select several pairs at a time.]	The children should identify what they like about each other's performances. Encourage them to describe how they feel when they are showing their sequences.

Apparatus

	Content	Teaching points
1	Individually explore the floor space by performing actions either strongly or lightly. When you come to the apparatus, find places where you need a lot of strength to climb, pull, or hang.	Verbalise the children's responses.
2	Start on a magic spot. Hold a low strong starting position. Travel lightly to the apparatus. Find somewhere on the apparatus where you can be strong by performing an action powerfully, or where you can hang. On the sound of the tambour, travel lightly back to your magic spot.	Select some children to demonstrate as part of a mini plenary so the rest of the class learn from the highlighted criteria discussed.

Cool-down/calming down
Do six strong jumps that gradually become lighter on the spot. Stretch up lightly and bend your body in half with a heavy movement. Hold still for the count of four.

Classroom
Identify what the children thought they did well and what they need to do to improve for the next lesson.

SESSION 8
Moving in different directions

Consolidation from previous session: to perform movements and/or actions either in a light or strong manner; to lift, carry and place equipment safely.

LEARNING OBJECTIVES

The objectives of the session need to be made explicit to the children. They also need to assess the extent to which they have achieved them.

Physical

1   To know the different directional terms (forwards, backwards, sideways and diagonally), and be able to apply these to actions.

2   To be able to remember and perform a sequence.

Well-being

3   To know that healthy eating and physical activity are beneficial to health and well-being.

Broader learning

4   To know how to give supportive feedback to a partner after a performance.

ASSESSMENT CRITERIA – QUESTIONS TO CONSIDER

1   Do the children understand directional instructions and are they able to apply them to their actions?

2   Can they repeat a sequence they have remembered?

3   Are they aware that both a healthy diet and being physically active are beneficial to health and well-being?

4   Are they able to give positive feedback to support one another when performing?

Warm-up

	Content	Teaching points
1	Travel around the room, on your tummy or back, pushing or pulling yourself using your arms.	Verbalise the children's responses.
2	Travel on your hands and feet, holding your bodies strong. On the sound of the tambour, make your movements light.	Reinforce the differences in where the children are applying their weight (for example, moving from using the whole foot to the toes).
3	Travel around on your hands and feet, and, on the sound of the tambour, spring up high.	Select one or two children to show and highlight the use of the arms to gain height.

Floor work

	Content	Teaching points
1	Do bouncy jumps and see if you can do these backwards. Now do bouncy jumps and go sideways. Now do bouncy jumps and travel diagonally.	Tell the children to look over their shoulders to check where they are going. Help with the term 'diagonally'.
2	Hold an interesting strong position and, on the sound of the tambour, take five bouncy jumps forwards and then jump on the spot for the count of five. Then, take five bouncy jumps backwards and continue for the count of five. Then, take five bouncy jumps sideways and continue for the count of five. Finally, take five bouncy jumps diagonally and continue for the count of five.	Help with the term 'diagonally' and select some children to demonstrate.
3	Hold a starting position but, this time, you decide which direction you are going to jump. Continue for the count of five, then change jumps, and so on.	Select some children to show and reinforce where they change direction, and which direction they choose.
4	Practise your sequence so you can remember it.	Give individual feedback.
5	Get into pairs and number yourselves 1 and 2. 2 should show 1 their sequence. Hold your starting position and start on 'go', then change places.	The children should tell their partner what they liked about their sequence.

Apparatus

	Content	Teaching points
1	Find a magic spot. Travel by jumping in different directions and, when you come to the apparatus, jump on to, over, along and off the apparatus in different directions. On the sound of the tambour, find a different way of travelling back to your magic spot.	Circulate and verbalise the responses (for example, 'Aisha is sliding backwards down the plank').

Cool-down/calming down
Walk quietly in and out of each other. Choose whether you go forwards, backwards or sideways. Then stand still. [*Encourage straight backs and good posture.*]

Classroom
Identify what the children thought they did well and what they need to do to improve for the next lesson.

Moving up, down and sideways

Consolidation from previous session: to travel in different directions (forwards, sideways, backwards and diagonally); to lift, carry and place equipment safely.

LEARNING OBJECTIVES

The objectives of the session need to be made explicit to the children. They also need to assess the extent to which they have achieved them.

Physical

1   To know that movements can be performed both at different levels and in different directions.

2   To be able work with a partner to produce a sequence that can be remembered and performed.

Well-being

3   To know that healthy eating and physical activity are beneficial to health and well-being.

Broader learning

4   To identify strengths and know how to improve.

ASSESSMENT CRITERIA – QUESTIONS TO CONSIDER

1   Can children perform their movements and actions at different levels and in different directions?

2   Can they work with a partner and perform a sequence that they have both remembered?

3   Are they aware that both a healthy diet and being physically active are beneficial to their health and well-being?

4   Can they talk about their strengths and know what they have to do to improve?

Warm-up

	Content	Teaching points
1	Jump in and out of each other, and, on the sound of the tambour, change direction.	Verbalise the children's responses.
2	Jump in and out of each other, and, on the sound of the tambour, change the level of your jump.	Select one or two children to show and highlight changes in level.
3	Jump in and out of each other, and, on the sound of the tambour, change the direction and the level of your jump.	Select one or two children to demonstrate, and highlight changes in both direction and level. If none are shown, select a child who will be able to show this.

Floor work

	Content	Teaching points
1	Start low near the floor, spring high, and finish low. Bend you knees when you land.	Emphasise slight 'give' in the knees on take-off and landing.
2	Can you do this again but, this time, travel sideways?	Select one or two children to demonstrate.
3	Do three jumps – one high in the air, then jump to your right, and then to your left.	Indicate right and left to the children. Remind them how to identify right and left using their hands.
4	With a partner, practise these movements together.	Provide time for the children to practise. Circulate and provide formative feedback. Ask the children to identify their strengths and what they want to improve.
5	In pairs, half the class should perform their sequences to the rest of class, and then change places.	Guide the children as to who they should watch, and ask them to identify what the children are doing well.

Apparatus

	Content	Teaching points
1	Start away from the apparatus on your magic spot. Travel on the floor using your jumping actions (jumping low to high to low). When you come to the apparatus, find places where you can travel sideways on to, along, over and off the apparatus. On the sound of the tambour, see if you can find another way of travelling back to your magic spot, using an action that you can start from low and stretch high.	Circulate and verbalise responses. Build up gradually. Choose a good example for the rest of the children to watch (mini plenary), and highlight your expectations. Discuss with the children what they saw.

Cool-down/calming down

Stand in a space, crouch down, stretch up high and then crouch down again. Do this several times, gradually getting slower, until you come to a stop.

Classroom

Identify what the children thought they did well and what they need to do to improve for the next lesson.

SESSION 10
Assessment activity

This session is for interim assessment. It assesses what children have learned in previous sessions so that the teacher can evaluate their progress and determine what needs to be reinforced in the next sessions. There is only floor work.

ASSESSMENT TASKS

On the floor

Combine three travelling actions that include one or more of the following: a change of speed/direction/level. Combine these actions with a starting body shape and finish with a rotation.

Practise, remember and perform the sequence.

DISCUSSION

Talk about what changes happen to the body when it is active, and the benefits of being active to your health and well-being.

Discuss your work and say what you might do to make it even better.

ASSESSMENT CRITERIA – QUESTIONS TO CONSIDER

1   Can the children perform three travelling actions in a sequence, showing a change of direction/speed/level?

2   Can they add a starting shape and add a rotation movement to complete their sequence?

3   Can they remember and perform the sequence with consistency, coordination and control?

4   Can they talk about the changes that happen to their bodies when they are active, and the benefits of being active to their health and well-being?

5   Can they talk about the new skills they have learned?

6   Can they identify actions/movements that they can perform well, and know one or two ways in which they can improve?

OUTCOME

Some children will achieve, some will excel and some will achieve less.

Warm-up

	Content	Teaching points
I	Play the 'Bean Game'. [See *Session 10 from Year 1, page 96.*]	Verbalise the children's body actions and highlight where they are demonstrating good control and tension.

Floor work

	Content	Teaching points
1	Remember all the different ways that you have travelled around the hall. On the sound of the tambour, change either the direction, speed or level of your movement.	Encourage the children to perform several different travelling actions and verbalise these. Draw attention to the variety of ways that actions/movements can be performed (for example, with a change of direction, speed or level). Select an example to show.
2	Explore a starting position that you can combine with your travelling action. Practise and refine.	Show and highlight interesting body shapes, good body tension, stretched toes and fingers, and so on. Ask the children what they can do well and what they need to do to improve.
3	Hold your starting position and, on the count of three, add your travelling action. Add another travelling action on a second count of three, and add another on a third count of three. Practise and refine so you remember the sequence.	Circulate and set differentiated challenges to accommodate individual abilities. For example, some children may be adding more movements/actions to their sequence. Select some children to demonstrate, and highlight interesting body shapes, good body tension, stretched toes and fingers, and smooth transition of movements.
4	Hold your starting position and, on the count of three, go through your sequence. This time, make sure you add a change in direction, level or speed. Practise and refine so you remember your sequence.	Select some children to demonstrate, and highlight changes in direction, speed and level.
5	Practise and refine these movements so you remember them. Can you add a rotation to the end of your sequence?	Select some children to demonstrate, and highlight interesting body shapes, good body tension, and smooth transition of travelling movements. Look also for changes of direction/speed/level, and encourage the children to use rotations to finish the sequence.
6	In pairs, name yourselves 1 and 2. 2 should show their sequence to 1, and then change places.	Encourage the children to identify whether their partner included three actions, a change of direction, level or speed, and finished their sequence with a rotation action.
	ASSESSMENT – By the teacher (in conjunction with a teaching assistant, where applicable), and also peer assessment by the children. Use ICT to record as many performances as possible so the children can self-assess during the lesson and in the classroom. This can also be kept as a record of their achievement.	

'Hands flat on the floor under shoulders, arms straight and both feet pushed into the air.'

'The children should describe their partner's movements.'

SESSION 11

Taking weight/holding still positions

Consolidation from previous session: to perform actions by springing high and low, and moving sideways; to lift, carry and place equipment safely.

LEARNING OBJECTIVES

The objectives of the session need to be made explicit to the children. They also need to assess the extent to which they have achieved them.

Physical

1   To demonstrate different balances on feet and hands.

2   To know how to balance on the apparatus in a variety of ways.

Well-being

3   To know that being active is good for health and well-being.

Broader learning

4   To know that, when working with a partner, it is important to share ideas.

ASSESSMENT CRITERIA – QUESTIONS TO CONSIDER

1   Can the children balance on their feet and hands in different ways?

2   Can they balance on the apparatus in a variety of ways?

3   Can they talk about some of the ways in which being active is beneficial to their health and well-being?

4   Are they able to share ideas when working with a partner?

Warm-up

	Content	Teaching points
1	Run in and out of each other, and, on the sound of the tambour, jump to the right and then to the left.	Verbalise the responses. Remind the children how to identify right and left using their hands.
2	Jump in and out of each other, and, on the sound of the tambour, spring high and finish low.	Emphasise slight 'give' in the knees on take-off and landing.
3	Choose how to move and, on the sound of the tambour, spring up high and finish low, or move sideways to the right or the left.	Select some children to demonstrate. Highlight good body tension, feet together when jumping, slight bending of knees on take-off and landing, and so on.

Floor work

	Content	Teaching points
1	Find a way of balancing on your hands and feet.	Discuss what we mean by balancing (keeping steady on a small base). Encourage good strong body tension.
2	Try to balance using two hands and one foot.	As above, discuss what we mean by balancing (keeping steady on a small base). Encourage good strong body tension.
3	Now balance using one hand and two feet.	As above, discuss what we mean by balancing (keeping steady on a small base). Encourage good strong body tension.
4	Now balance using one hand and one foot.	As above, discuss what we mean by balancing (keeping steady on a small base). Encourage good strong body tension.
5	Choose one of these balances, and, on the count of four, change your balance, and hold for a further count of four.	As above, discuss what we mean by balancing (keeping steady on a small base). Encourage good strong body tension.
6	With a partner, practise putting two balances together. Can you manage three? Now show each other your sequence and tell your partner something you like about their sequence. Talk about what you would like to improve in your own sequence.	Choose some examples for the class to watch. Ask what parts are being used to balance on.

Apparatus

	Content	Teaching points
1	Find a magic spot and hold a balance. Hold for the count of four. Travel up to the apparatus in an interesting way and find places where you can hold interesting balances. Travel back to your magic spot in a different interesting way.	Circulate and verbalise responses (for example, 'James is balancing on the bench on his hands and one foot').

Cool-down/calming down
Find a space to balance on two feet and two hands. Hold for the count of four and stretch out a foot for the count of four. Place the foot down and stretch out an arm for the count of four. Now, stretch out an arm and a leg. Hold for the count of four, and slowly lie flat on to the ground and hold your body still.

Classroom
Identify what the children thought they did well and what they need to do to improve for the next lesson.

Transferring weight: feet to hands (1)

Consolidation from previous session: to take weight on feet and hands in different combinations while still; to lift, carry and place equipment safely.

LEARNING OBJECTIVES

The objectives of the session need to be made explicit to the children. They also need to assess the extent to which they have achieved them.

Physical

1   To know how to take weight on hands and feet in a variety of ways.

2   To know what is meant by 'distributing weight'.

Well-being

3   To be aware that some substances are harmful to the body.

Broader learning

4   To know how to share their ideas with one another and know why it is important to be able to do so.

ASSESSMENT CRITERIA – QUESTIONS TO CONSIDER

1   Can the children perform actions where they take their weight on their hands?

2   Can they transfer their weight from feet to hands, and hands to feet?

3   Are they able to talk about substances that are harmful to the body?

4   Can they share their ideas with their peers?

Warm-up

	Content	Teaching points
1	Run in and out of each other, and, on the sound of the tambour, take your weight on two feet and two hands.	Encourage the children to have straight arms and legs, and good body tension.
2	Jump in and out of each other, and, on the sound of the tambour, take your weight on two hands and one foot.	Encourage the children to jump while keeping their feet together, taking off and landing with their knees slightly bent.
3	Skip in and out of each other, and, on the sound of the tambour, take your weight on one hand and one foot. Move with control into the held position.	Verbalise the children's responses.
4	Choose how to move around the room and, on sound of the tambour, hold a balance.	Select one or two examples to show and highlight the above key teaching points.

Floor work

	Content	Teaching points
1	Practise bunny hops.	Emphasise hands flat on the floor under shoulders, arms straight and both feet pushed into the air (see 'Specific skills guide', page 169).
2	Do bunny hops and, on the count of four, change direction. Now try them forwards, backwards, sideways and diagonally.	Ask the children to do this several times.
3	Now do one-handed bunny hops and then use the other hand.	Encourage children to take weight on just one hand.
4	Now do bunny hops using two hands and one foot.	Encourage children to take weight securely on both hands.
5	Find a way of going from your feet to your hands, and back again to your feet.	Make sure the children's weight is put on their hands. Discuss what is meant by transferring weight. Choose one or two children to demonstrate.
6	Hold a starting position and then transfer your weight from your feet to your hands, and then back again.	With a partner, tell them when your weight is on your feet, hands or equally divided between the two.

Apparatus

	Content	Teaching points
1	Use the floor to explore taking weight on your hands and feet. When you come to the apparatus, explore where you can bunny hop on to, along, over and off the apparatus.	Verbalise the children's responses.
2	Find a magic spot and travel up to the apparatus by doing bunny hops, forwards, backwards, sideways or diagonally. Then, move along or over the apparatus by doing bunny hops, where possible, and return to your magic spot.	Select one or two examples to show the children.

Cool-down/calming down
Stretch up high, reaching up to the ceiling with your fingertips, standing on your tiptoes. Gradually roll your body down towards the floor into a tight ball.

Classroom
Identify what the children thought they did well and what they need to do to improve for the next lesson.

Transferring weight: feet to hands (2)

Consolidation from previous session: to perform bunny hops (forwards, sideways, backwards and diagonally); to lift, carry and place equipment safely.

LEARNING OBJECTIVES

The objectives of the session need to be made explicit to the children. They also need to assess the extent to which they have achieved them.

Physical

1   To know how to take weight on hands and feet to form a cartwheel shape.

2   To know how to transfer weight from one hand to another on apparatus.

Well-being

3   To know that other factors contribute to health and well-being in addition to being active.

Broader learning

4   To identify what they do well and what they have to do to improve.

ASSESSMENT CRITERIA – QUESTIONS TO CONSIDER

1   Can the children perform a mini cartwheel action (legs may be bent at this stage)?

2   Can they transfer their weight from one hand to the other across a bench?

3   Can they talk about other factors that contribute to their health and well-being?

4   Can they discuss what they can do well and how to improve?

Warm-up

	Content	Teaching points
1	Do bunny hops in and out of each other. On the sound of the tambour, change direction.	Verbalise the children's responses.
2	Do bunny hops by travelling forwards. On the sound of the tambour, change to either bunny hopping backwards, sideways or diagonally.	Demonstrate a diagonal bunny hop using a child as a model.
3	Do bunny hops around the hall but, this time, you choose when to change direction or speed.	Select one or two children to show their ideas.

Floor work

	Content	Teaching points
1	In pairs, practise your bunny hops. Check that your partner is taking weight on their hands correctly.	Emphasise flat hands (fingers spread).

	Content	Teaching points
2	Find other ways of going from your feet to your hands, and back to your feet again.	Encourage the children to keep their arms straight and to avoid overbalancing by moving one hand forward. Balance on the apparatus for the count of three.
3	Place one hand on the floor and jump your feet up to that hand. Then, place your other hand on the floor and jump your feet up to it again.	Talk about cartwheels, explaining the spokes of a wheel (see 'Specific skills guide', page 169).
4	Place one hand on the floor, then place the other hand on the floor ahead of it, then jump your feet so you land close to the second hand.	See 'Specific skills guide' (page 169).
5	Do this again, turning round as you go.	Choose a child who is doing this correctly to model.
6	Do this again, but land one foot after the other.	These are mini cartwheels – legs may be bent at this stage. Circulate to give formative feedback, and encourage the children to straighten their legs.

Apparatus – using benches and a mat

	Content	Teaching points
1	Walk up to the bench and place one hand on the near side, followed by the other on the opposite side, and kick your legs over.	Choose a child doing this correctly to model.
2	Do the same again, but try to straighten your legs.	Emphasise using strength in the arms to assist in holding the legs straight (this sounds strange but it works).

Floor work

	Content	Teaching points
1	Now return to a space on the floor and try the same action.	Select some children to demonstrate, and identify the well-executed actions.

Cool-down/calming down
Take your weight on your hands and kick up high, then not so high, and finally kick up just off the floor. Hug your knees and sit down quietly.

Classroom
Identify what the children thought they did well and what they need to do to improve for the next lesson.

SESSION 14
Transferring body weight

Consolidation from previous session: to perform bunny hops and transfer weight from hand to hand to form a cartwheel shape; to lift, carry and place equipment safely.

LEARNING OBJECTIVES

The objectives of the session need to be made explicit to the children. They also need to assess the extent to which they have achieved them.

Physical

1   To know how to balance on different body parts.

2   To be able to devise a sequence that can be remembered.

Well-being

3   To be able to identify how the body feels after being active.

Broader learning

4   To listen to and show consideration for the views of a partner.

ASSESSMENT CRITERIA – QUESTIONS TO CONSIDER

1   Can the children perform a variety of balances?

2   Can they devise and repeat short compositions?

3   Can they describe how they feel after activity?

4   Can they work with a partner, listening and sharing ideas?

Warm-up

	Content	Teaching points
1	Move around the hall in and out of each other, taking your weight on your hands with your tummy either facing the floor or the ceiling. When you hear the tambour, change so that your tummy is pointing in the opposite direction.	Select some children to demonstrate. Highlight good body tension and straight arms.
2	Bunny hop around the hall and, on the count of three, change the direction of your hop to either sideways, backwards or diagonally. Do this several times.	Verbalise changes (for example, 'Navanja is moving sideways by placing her hand on the floor, across from her body, and taking the weight on her hands'). Select two or three children to demonstrate.

	Content	Teaching points
3	Transfer your weight from one hand to another to make a cartwheel shape.	Select a child who can perform a cartwheel, and draw attention to transferring weight from one hand to the other, starting and finishing facing the same direction, the position of the hips, and straight legs.
4	Decide how to travel on your hands around the room and, on the sound of the tambour, either change action or direction.	Verbalise some of the responses.

Floor work

	Content	Teaching points
1	Use different parts of your body to balance on.	This is revision of the ideas from Session 11 (page 60).
2	Balance on your bottom, and then turn and balance on your tummy. Try not to let any other part of your body touch the floor.	Encourage the children to hold strong body tension while balancing.
3	Use part of your body to balance on, and then move smoothly into another balance.	Select one or two children to demonstrate, and highlight how one action moves into another with minimal effort.
4	Use a part of your body to balance on, and then turn or lean over in order to balance on a different part.	As above, select one or two children to demonstrate, and highlight how one action moves into another with minimal effort.
5	With a partner, name yourselves 1 and 2. 2 should hold a body shape and, on 'go', move into a balance, hold for the count of three, turn or lean, and hold a further balance for the count of three. Then, change places.	Encourage smooth transitions, using some children to demonstrate. The children should describe their partner's movements.

Apparatus

	Content	Teaching points
1	Start on your magic spot. Find a way to travel towards the apparatus on your hands and feet, changing your movement on each count of three. Balance on the apparatus for the count of three and see if you can change smoothly from your balance into a different balance. Travel back to your magic spot and hold a finishing balance on your spot for the count of three.	Build this up gradually. Select a good example for the rest of the class to watch. Discuss with the children what they have seen. Circulate and suggest parts of the body to balance on.

Cool-down/calming down

In your space, do a shoulder balance (legs straight and stretched above the head, weight on the shoulders and the top part of the spine, hands supporting the body at the waist). Can you hold your legs still for the count of three, and gradually roll down and curl up?

Classroom

Identify what the children thought they did well and what they need to do to improve for the next lesson.

'Independently, find ways to slide on to, under, over, along and off the apparatus.'

'See where you can travel on to, along, over and off the apparatus with feet together and feet apart.'

SESSION 15
Jumping and landing with feet either together or apart

Consolidation from previous session: to move from one balance into another; to lift, carry and place equipment safely.

LEARNING OBJECTIVES

The objectives of the session need to be made explicit to the children. They also need to assess the extent to which they have achieved them.

Physical

1   To develop the control and coordination of gymnastics movements.

2   To improve performance by observation.

Well-being

3   To recognise how it feels to receive feedback from others.

Broader learning

4   To identify the help required in order to develop floor work and apparatus work.

ASSESSMENT CRITERIA – QUESTIONS TO CONSIDER

1   Can the children demonstrate good body control and coordination in their movements?

2   Can they observe each other and identify good coordination and control?

3   Can they respond positively to feedback?

4   Can they articulate the help they require in order to improve their work?

Warm-up

	Content	Teaching points
1	Hold a balance and, on the sound of the tambour, run, skip or jump in and out of each other. On two strikes of the tambour, hold a balance on a different body part. Repeat this several times.	Verbalise movement actions and balances (for example, 'Jenny is balancing on her shoulders, holding her legs straight and stretching her toes').
2	Hold a balance and, on the sound of the tambour, run, skip or jump in and out of each other. On two strikes of the tambour, hold a balance for the count of three and then move smoothly into another balance on a different body part. Repeat this several times.	Select two or three children to demonstrate, and encourage the rest of the class to describe the actions.
3	Select your own way of moving around the hall and choose when to hold a balance and move again.	Encourage strong control in the children's stillness.

Floor work

	Content	Teaching points
1	Practise star jumps.	The children should start with their feet together, part them in the air and bring them together on landing.
2	Do light bouncy jumps with your feet together. Soft knees on landing.	The children should use their arms to lift up high.
3	Do three light bouncy jumps and one star jump.	The children should use their arms to lift up high and then stretch them out.
4	Hold a balance as a starting position for the count of three, then do three light bouncy jumps and a star jump.	The children should count out loud, and think about when they will change their action.
5	Practise and this time you decide how many star jumps and bouncy jumps to include. Practise so you know your sequence.	Select a few examples for the rest of the class to watch. Discuss what makes a good movement phrase.
6	Show a partner your sequence. Discuss what you did well and what you want to improve and ask your partner to assess you against the given criteria.	Help out with the criteria (for example, variety, control, high jumps and so on).

Apparatus

	Content	Teaching points
1	Start on your magic spot. Travel up to the apparatus doing light bouncy jumps and/or star jumps. When you get to the apparatus, find ways of jumping on, along, over and off the apparatus performing either of these jumps. On the sound of the tambour, travel back to your magic spot.	Build this up gradually. Select an example for the class to watch. Discuss when the feet should be apart and when they should be together.

Cool-down/calming down

On the spot, jump high with your feet together and then do a star jump. Curl your body up tightly when you land and slowly, for the count of six, roll your body into a tight ball on the floor.

Classroom

Identify what the children thought they did well and what they need to do to improve for the next lesson.

Travelling on hands and feet, with feet either together or apart

Consolidation from previous session: to jump with feet apart or together; to lift, carry and place equipment safely.

LEARNING OBJECTIVES

The objectives of the session need to be made explicit to the children. They also need to assess the extent to which they have achieved them.

Physical

1   To improve performance using particular criteria for the evaluation.

2   To devise a sequence with a partner.

Well-being

3   To identify the new skills they have learned.

Broader learning

4   To identify their own and others' strengths.

ASSESSMENT CRITERIA – QUESTIONS TO CONSIDER

1   Can the children explain and apply what they have to do to improve their movements?

2   Can they work out a movement sequence with a partner that they can remember and perform?

3   Can they identify the new skills they have learned?

4   Can they describe their own and others' strengths?

Warm-up

	Content	Teaching points
1	Do light bouncy jumps in and out of each other around the hall. On the sound of the tambour, do a big springy jump.	Reinforce legs bent on take-off and landing.
2	Do light bouncy jumps in and out of each other around the hall. On the sound of the tambour, do a star jump.	The children should start with their feet together, part them in the air, and bring them together on landing.
3	Choose how you want to jump in and out of each other around the hall, and, on the sound of the tambour, change your jumping action.	Select good examples for the rest of the class to watch.

Floor work

	Content	Teaching points
1	Find a way of travelling using your hands and feet. Keep your feet together as you go.	Discuss different ways of doing this first and then verbalise the children's responses.
2	Now try to travel the same way but have your feet apart.	As above, discuss different ways of doing this first and then verbalise the children's responses.
3	Travel on your hands and feet in different ways. Sometimes have your feet together and sometimes have them apart.	Look at some examples. The children should tell you when feet are together or apart.
4	Practise mini cartwheels with a partner. Watch each other and describe what each other is doing.	See Session 13 (page 150) and 'Specific skills guide' (page 169).
5	Together, work out a sequence that includes some of the movements you have been doing.	Circulate and provide formative feedback. Half of the class should watch the other half and then change over. Ensure the children watch only one or two pairs. The children should observe and provide feedback against given criteria (the children could decide on these).

Apparatus

	Content	Teaching points
1	Find a magic spot. Hold a balance for the count of three and travel on the floor with your feet together or apart. Change your actions so that your tummy is sometimes facing the floor and sometimes the ceiling. See where you can travel on to, along, over and off the apparatus with feet together and feet apart. On the sound of the tambour, return to your magic spot doing light bouncy jumps.	Select an example for the class to watch. Ask the children to identify where feet were together and where they were apart.

Cool-down/calming down
Stretch up and hold the stretch for the count of three. Jump up with your feet apart and then jump up with your feet together. Finally, jump and land down low, spinning on your bottom and tucking up tightly.

Classroom
Identify what the children thought they did well and what they need to do to improve for the next lesson.

SESSION 17

Sliding and rolling, with feet either together or apart

Consolidation from previous session: to travel with feet together or apart; to lift, carry and place equipment safely.

LEARNING OBJECTIVES

The objectives of the session need to be made explicit to the children. They also need to assess the extent to which they have achieved them.

Physical

1   To develop skills of rolling and sliding.

2   To use criteria and observation to develop the rolls.

Well-being

3   To know that a healthy diet is important for health and well-being.

Broader learning

4   To know how to perform actions safely and with consideration for others.

ASSESSMENT CRITERIA – QUESTIONS TO CONSIDER

1   Can the children roll in stretched and tucked positions?

2   Can they identify some of the criteria to develop their rolls?

3   Do they know which foods contribute positively to their health and well-being?

4   Can they explain why it is important to have enough space in which to perform?

Warm-up

	Content	Teaching points
1	Hold your weight on your hands and feet and, keeping your hands on the same spot, jump your feet in one direction. On the sound of the tambour, change so you are jumping in the other direction. Keep your feet together.	Select one or two children to demonstrate. Emphasise flat hands pressing hard into the floor.
2	Now do the same again, but keep your feet apart.	As above, select one or two children to demonstrate. Emphasise flat hands pressing hard into the floor.
3	Now move around the room taking the weight from hands to feet. On the sound of the tambour, keep your hands on the same spot and jump your feet around your body.	Demonstrate or select some children to demonstrate these movements.
4	Choose whether to jump with your feet apart or together, and when to keep your hands on the same spot, and jump your feet around your body.	Articulate the different responses seen.

Floor work

	Content	Teaching points
1	Get out mats. On a mat, roll sideways, tucked up with your feet together.	Discourage covering the eyes.
2	On a mat, roll sideways, stretched out with your feet apart.	The children should be fully stretched, holding legs slightly off the floor.
3	On a mat, stretch, tuck, and stretch as you roll.	As above, the children should be fully stretched, with strong tension in the centre of the body.
4	On the floor, slide with your feet together.	Some children can slide while others are still rolling on the mats.
5	Slide with your feet apart.	The children should hold strong body tension.
6	Hold a starting balance and then, with a partner, make up a phrase to include rolling and sliding. Sometimes have your feet together and sometimes apart.	Give formative feedback to the pairs as they are working. Encourage the use of the floor and the mats.
7	A few pairs at a time should show their sequences and the other groups should say what they like.	Articulate good practice and encourage the children to set themselves a goal.

Apparatus

	Content	Teaching points
1	With your partner, start on your magic spot. Perform your rolling and sliding movement phrase up to the apparatus and, independently, find ways to slide on to, under, over, along and off the apparatus. Roll on the mat before you travel back to your magic spot, in any way you choose.	Build this up gradually. Circulate to make suggestions.

Cool-down/calming down

Sit on the floor in a space. Spin around in one direction on the spot and then the other. Curl up and hold you body in a curled, tight position for the count of three. Gradually release the tension so you are sitting upright with legs crossed.

Classroom

Identify what the children thought they did well and what they need to do to improve for the next lesson.

SESSION 18

Travelling along straight lines

Consolidation from previous session: to slide and roll sideways, with feet apart and together; to lift, carry and place equipment safely.

LEARNING OBJECTIVES

The objectives of the session need to be made explicit to the children. They also need to assess the extent to which they have achieved them.

Physical

1   To be able to control and coordinate actions while moving in a straight line.

2   To use criteria and observation to develop sequences.

Well-being

3   To know clearly some of the benefits of physical activity to health and well-being.

Broader learning

4   To negotiate and collaborate in order to devise a sequence of movements.

ASSESSMENT CRITERIA – QUESTIONS TO CONSIDER

1   Can the children perform actions with control and coordination while moving in a straight line?

2   Can they identify some of the criteria against which to develop their actions?

3   Can they talk articulately about the benefits of engaging in an active lifestyle?

4   Can they share ideas, show their movements to one another and negotiate what movements to select to form a sequence together?

Warm-up

	Content	Teaching points
1	Run in and out of each other, and on the sound of the tambour, roll sideways with your feet together.	Select a child to watch, and highlight good body tension, straight legs and stretched arms.
2	Jump in and out of each other, and, on the sound of the tambour, slide with your feet together or apart.	Emphasise smooth transitions.
3	Skip in and out of each other, and, on the sound of the tambour, either roll or slide.	The children should decide which to do before they move close to the floor.

Floor work

	Content	Teaching points
1	Find a way of travelling along a straight line using your feet in an interesting way.	Talk about how tightrope walkers achieve this.
2	Travel along a straight line on your hands and feet.	Encourage the children to remember previously learned skills (for example, bunny hops and cartwheels).
3	Find ways of travelling along a straight line using other parts of your body.	Verbalise the responses.
4	With a partner, show each other your movement ideas and select two or three of them. Practise putting them together in a sequence.	Encourage the children to add a starting position. You may need to build up gradually and differentiate here. Encourage children to make up a phrase moving in a straight line, and then turning to go along another line.
5	Now we will show each other our sequences. [*Several pairs at a time.*]	Tell the children who they should be watching and to look out for specific aspects relating to the criteria set.

Apparatus

	Content	Teaching points
1	Find a magic spot and, on 'go', travel individually in a straight line towards the apparatus. Find places where you can travel straight up, down and along the apparatus. On the sound of the tambour, travel back to your magic spot using a different action.	Circulate and make suggestions. Select one or two children to show as a mini plenary, and then give the children several more turns so that they can refine their ideas and actions.

Cool-down/calming down
Walk tall in a straight line. Gradually get nearer to the ground so that, by the count of eight, you are as close to the ground as possible.

Classroom
Identify what the children thought they did well and what they need to do to improve for the next lesson.

SESSION 19

Travelling using zigzag pathways

Consolidation from previous session: to travel in a straight line in a variety of ways; to lift, carry and place equipment safely.

LEARNING OBJECTIVES

The objectives of the session need to be made explicit to the children. They also need to assess the extent to which they have achieved them.

Physical

1   To be able to control and coordinate actions using a zigzag pathway.
2   To use criteria and observation to develop sequences.

Well-being

3   To identify what is good in a partner's performance and share this together.

Broader learning

4   To work with another person cooperatively.

ASSESSMENT CRITERIA – QUESTIONS TO CONSIDER

1   Can the children perform actions with control and coordination using a zigzag pathway?
2   Can they identify some of the criteria against which to develop their actions?
3   Can they observe each other and give positive supportive feedback?
4   Are they demonstrating some skills for working collaboratively with each other?

Warm-up

	Content	Teaching points
1	Walk in and out of each other in straight lines, and, when I strike the tambour, turn, change direction and walk in a straight line again.	Verbalise the responses – emphasise good posture.
2	Run in and out of each other in straight lines, and, when I strike the tambour, turn, change direction and run in a straight line again.	This requires the children to have a good sense of how far they can run and not collide.
3	Jump in and out of each other in straight lines, and, when I strike the tambour, turn, change direction and jump in a straight line again.	Highlight knees bent slightly on take-off and landing.
4	Skip in and out of each other in straight lines, and, when I strike the tambour, turn, change direction and skip in a straight line again.	The children should use their arms to lift in the skips.
5	Choose how to move, and when to turn and change direction. On the sound of the tambour, change your movement action.	Verbalise the responses.

Floor work

	Content	Teaching points
1	Do bouncy jumps along a zigzag pathway.	Discuss the term 'zigzag' first.
2	Use your hands and feet to travel along a zigzag pathway.	Remind the children about the different actions they might use (from previous sessions).
3	Find other parts of your body to travel on along a zigzag pathway.	As above, remind the children about the different actions they might use (from previous sessions).
4	With a partner, show your different actions and select three to combine in a sequence.	Give the children time to practise, refine, evaluate and perform.
5	Add a starting position to your sequence. Now we will show each other our sequences.	Half the class should show the rest of the class their sequences, and then change places. Direct individual pairs to watch each other and give them criteria to assess against. Ask them to say what they like about the other pair's performance.

Apparatus

	Content	Teaching points
1	Find a magic spot. Travel up to the apparatus taking a zigzag pathway. Move on to, along and over the apparatus any way you choose. On the sound of the tambour, choose a different way to return to your magic spot.	Circulate and make suggestions. Select one or two children to demonstrate as a mini plenary, and then give the children several more turns so that they can refine their ideas and actions.

Cool-down/calming down
Walk in a zigzag pathway, slowly changing it into a straight line to the count of eight.

Classroom
Identify what the children thought they did well and what they need to do to improve for the next lesson.

SESSION 20
Assessment activity

This session has the final assessment tasks for Key Stage 1. It assesses what the children have learned across both Year 1 and Year 2.

Teachers should identify the stage of development at which each child is consistently working (early, middle and later) so that this information can be transferred to Year 3, and the children can continue to build on what they have already learned. This session includes both floor and apparatus work.

ASSESSMENT TASKS

On the floor

Combine three travelling actions that include one or more of the following: a change of speed/direction/level.

Add to this by including a starting body shape and finishing movement.

Practise, remember and perform the sequence.

On the apparatus

Transfer your travelling actions/movements from the floor on to the apparatus (for example, start on the floor, move towards the apparatus and then either travel on to, along, over or off, using one or more of your movements). Finish with a rotation action.

DISCUSSION

Explain what you must do to stay healthy and well.

Talk about what is good work and say what you might do to make it even better.

ASSESSMENT CRITERIA – QUESTIONS TO CONSIDER

1   Can the children perform three travelling actions in a sequence showing a change of direction/speed/level?

2   Can they add a starting shape and a rotation movement to complete their sequence?

3   Can they remember and perform the sequence with consistency, coordination and control?

4   Can they talk about the changes that happen to their bodies when they are active, and the benefits of being active to their health and well-being?

5   Can they identify actions/movements that they can perform well, and know one or two ways in which they can improve?

OUTCOME

Some children will achieve, some will excel and some will achieve less.

Warm-up

	Content	Teaching points
1	Play the 'Bean Game'. [*See Session 10 from Year 1, page 96.*]	Verbalise the children's body actions, and highlight where they are demonstrating with good control and tension.

Floor work

	Content	Teaching points
1	Select a starting position and, on the sound of the tambour, add two travelling actions to make a sequence.	Encourage the children to perform several different travelling actions and verbalise these. Encourage them to perform each travelling action for the count of three.
2	Practise and refine, and, when you can remember your sequence, add another movement to it.	Circulate and set differentiated challenges to accommodate individual abilities (for example, some children may be adding more movements/actions to their sequence). Select some children to demonstrate, and draw attention to the variety of ways that actions/movements can be performed (for example, with a change of direction, speed and level. Ask the children what they can do well and what they need to do to improve.
3	Consider how you are going to finish your sequence. Try to remember all the movements you have performed in previous lessons and select one of these.	Select some children to demonstrate, and highlight previously performed actions (for example, where children are taking weight on different body parts, taking zigzag pathways, rotating or spinning, sliding, pulling, pushing, and so on).
4	In pairs name yourselves 1 and 2. 2 should show 1 their sequence, and then change places.	Encourage the children to identify whether their partner included three actions, a change of direction, level or speed, and a finishing action.

Apparatus

	Content	Teaching points
1	In pairs, find a space in the hall and hold your starting position. On the sound of the tambour, perform your sequence on the floor and apparatus.	Verbalise the range of responses. The children should watch their partner and say what is good about the work. The performer should then identify an area that they would like to develop further.
	ASSESSMENT – By the teacher (in conjunction with a teaching assistant where applicable), and also peer assessment by the children. Use ICT to record as many performances as possible so the children can self-assess during the lesson and in the classroom. This can also be kept as a record of their achievement.	

Cool-down/calming down

Walk around the room, stretch up high and curl up tightly. Wait until you are tapped and then line up. [*Enrol some children to help.*]

Classroom

Look at some recordings of children's performances and discuss good practice. In pairs, the children should talk about what they did well and what they need to do to improve their performances. Can they record this?

Specific skills guide

Running

Running is an activity that is seldom taught, and which is used mainly for warm-up purposes. Few children, as a result, run well, that is in a mechanically efficient manner.

Children should be taught to bend their arms up, loosely clench their fists and use a pumping action with their arms to drive the body along. They should bend at the knees and emphasise a high knee lift. They should look where they are going, and be taught how to use their feet and twist their shoulders, to swerve and dodge in and out of other children when running.

Stopping

Children need to be able to stop suddenly. They should be taught to stop with one foot in front of the other, gripping tightly with their arm, leg and tummy muscles, and bending their knees slightly.

Jumping and landing

Children need to feel the strong thrust upwards through the legs and feet to get height. This can be increased with a vigorous swinging of the arms.

When jumping off something, the children should be taught a 'squashy' landing at first, bending the knees on impact in a deep squat position. Mats should be used and the children told to land in the middle of the mat, and encouraged to land on feet only. The hands may be placed in front of the body after landing, if more support is needed at first, but this should be discouraged as soon as is practicable. The children must land on both feet at once.

When jumping on the floor, a more resilient landing can be used like a bouncing ball. There is a slight give in the knees on landing, and then the body weight is reflected back up again (see Figure 1).

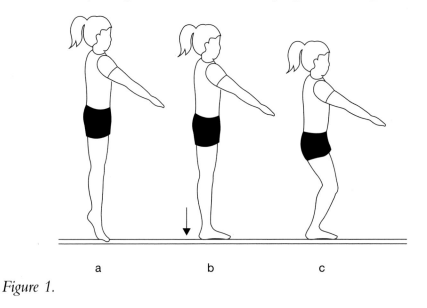

a   b   c

Figure 1.

Rolling

Mats should be used for rolling actions.

Children should first experience a rolling action by turning their body over sideways – 'rolling like a pencil down a hill'. They can also roll sideways, tucked up 'like a hedgehog', their knees and elbows touching. Their hands should not cover the face.

Forward rolls should not be taught as a class activity in Key Stage 1.

If they are taught at all this should be only on a one-to-one basis as follows:

Children should be shown how to crouch at the end of the mat, feet slightly apart. The hands are placed on the mat and the hips raised. If the knees are parted, the children can then be told to look 'backwards, through the window' (tuck their heads in as closely to the knees as possible). They can push themselves over onto their backs, reaching forward with their hands to regain standing (see Figure 2).

For further instruction and other ways of rolling see 'Specific skills guide' in the second volume, *Developing Physical Health and Well-being Through Gymnastics (7–11)*, third edition.

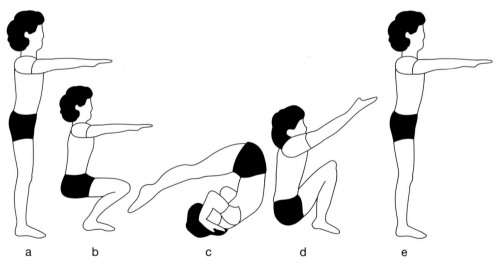

a   b   c   d   e

Figure 2.

Cartwheels

This is a safe activity for children because the weight is being transferred sideways and not forwards, as in a handstand. Infants can be taught to do 'mini cartwheels' as a class activity, and proper cartwheels may be attempted by individual children as a result. The following stages will assist in the skill development.

Stage 1: Bunny hops

The hands should be placed flat on the floor in front of the body. Arms should be straight.

Feet should be tucked up under the body.

Both feet should come off the floor and land simultaneously.

The children should travel about the room saying 'hands, feet' to get the correct transference of weight.

Stage 2: Crouch jumps

As for bunny hops, but on the spot, with emphasis on getting the hips up over the hands.

Children should be shown how to move on their hands, and to shift the weight in the event of the hips passing too far over the line of the inverted body, thus bringing the feet down safely to the starting place.

Care should be taken to ensure the children are spaced out and that there is no likelihood of a child getting kicked.

Stage 3: Starting to turn

Children can experiment with bringing the feet down to different places on the floor.

By placing the hands slightly to the side of the body and bringing the feet down beyond them, the body will have turned through an angle of 180 degrees. The teacher should try to identify those children who turn to the right and those who turn to the left.

Stage 4: The wheeling action

Talk to the children about wheels and spokes. Explain that the arms and legs are like the spokes of a wheel.

The children can try to start the turning action by putting one hand down after the other. Those turning to the right should put the right hand down followed by the left, and vice versa.

At this stage, the legs can remain bent and both feet can be brought down together.

They can then concentrate on bringing one foot down after the other. It helps if they say, 'foot, hand, hand, foot, foot' as they move (the first step on to the foot is important for future development of the cartwheel).

The teacher needs to watch that they get the sequencing right (right foot, right hand, left hand, left foot, right foot or vice versa).

Stage 5: The wheeling action with straight legs

Once they get the action right, providing the hips are lifted high, the children can concentrate on straightening the legs. They are now ready to attempt a correct cartwheel (see Figure 3 and also 'Specific skills guide' in the second volume, *Developing Physical Health and Well-being Through Gymnastics (7–11)*, third edition.

In the second volume, there is a more detailed 'Specific skills guide', with notes and diagrams for teaching:

- handstands;
- headstands;
- backwards rolls;
- jumping and landing (including the hurdle step); and
- round offs;
- simple variations in rolling.

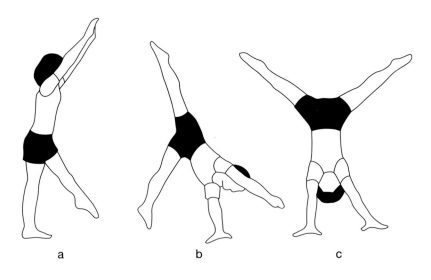

Figure 3.

SPECIFIC SKILLS GUIDE

2nd Edition

Developing Physical Health and Well-being Through Gymnastic Activity (7-11)
A Session-by-Session Approach

Maggie Carroll and Jackie Hannay

This companion volume to *Developing Physical Health and Well-being through Gymnastic Activity 5-7* follows the same format, and together, these user-friendly books provide a progressive programme of work from Years 1-6.

If you are a practising or student teacher, these books will give you all the confidence you need to teach gymnastics in your school!

<u>Book Details</u>
Developing Physical Health and Well-being through Gymnastic Activity (7-11)
A Session-by-Session Approach
October 2011: 246x189: 176pp
Pb: 978-0-415-59108-9: **£19.99**

To order:
Post: Education Marketing, 2 Park Square, Milton Park, Abingdon, OX14 4RN
Tel: 01235 400524
Fax: 020 7017 6699
Website: www.routledge.com/teachers

 Routledge
Taylor & Francis Group

www.routledge.com/teachers

The Really Useful Physical Education Book

Learning and Teaching across the 7–14 Age Range
The Really Useful Series

Edited by **Gary Stidder** and **Sid Hayes**

The Really Useful Physical Education Book provides training and practising teachers with guidance and ideas to teach physical education effectively and imaginatively across the 7-14 age range. It is underpinned by easy-to-understand theory and links to the curriculum and presents a wide range of high quality, fun lessons alongside engaging teaching examples and methodologies.

Book Details
The Really Useful Physical Education Book
Learning and Teaching across the 7–14 Age Range
July 2010: A4: 216pp
Pb: 978-0-415-49827-2: **£23.99**

To order:
Post: Education Marketing, 2 Park Square, Milton Park, Abingdon, OX14 4RN
Tel: 01235 400524
Fax: 020 7017 6699
Website: www.routledge.com/teachers

Routledge
Taylor & Francis Group

www.routledge.com/teachers